A handbook of ART TECHNIQUES

Roy Sparkes

BATSFORD ACADEMIC AND
EDUCATIONAL LIMITED London

First published 1981
© Roy Sparkes 1981

Printed in Great Britain by
Redwood Burn Ltd Trowbridge & Esher
for the publishers
Batsford Academic and Educational Limited
an imprint of B.T. Batsford.
4 Fitzhardinge Street, London W1H OAH

ISBN 0 7134 3386 8

Contents

Acknowledgment

I wish to express my thanks to all those colleagues and friends who have helped in the compilation of this book. My special gratitude goes to my family and close friends who have given encouragement and have been patiently kind; and to Thelma M Nye, whose idea the book was, for her advice and understanding.

Frindsbury, Kent, 1981   RS

Introduction

Here is an attempt to bring together those art techniques which can be explored without too much expense using readily available materials and equipment, and which, with care, can give great satisfaction. The list is not exhaustive and concentrates mainly on two-dimensional techniques. Well known methods are included, but there are also suggestions for exploring new ways of using the materials. Experimenting with different techniques is seen as important, for it helps the student to appreciate the potential of the equipment as well as to acquire new skills.

The acquisition of skills is twofold: firstly it involves getting to know and understanding materials; and secondly gaining control in using them. These two principles apply to all of the processes outlined in the following pages.

It is possible for all age groups, and all abilities, from beginners to professionals, to enjoy working with the techniques described here. Suggestions that certain materials and processes will facilitate spontaneity are not intended to imply that speed is preferable to careful working. The introduction of techniques should depend on the student's experience, understanding and capabilities in using the materials available. It is important to provide opportuntities for creating art work with a wide range of materials. The individual needs to be able to choose the medium he feels will best express his feelings. The disciplines which a particular medium imposes on an individual's attempt at using it will exercise a control over this expression.

Technical control should include a natural response and development of a realization of individual feelings and ideas in using the chosen medium. The latter will most probably come from experimenting, responding, discovering and organizing, with guidance where necessary. Where satisfaction is found in the use of one (or more) of the techniques, it is hoped that it will be explored and developed. Further information on techniques can be found in the technical notes and by reference to the Bibliography. Cross references are made in the text which may suggest developments of the techniques or alternative ways of working with the same equipment.

With all of the ideas suggested here, full expression is possible using the equipment in a controlled situation. This can lead to a sense of satisfaction from being involved in worthwhile activities, and an awareness of personal responsibility, and control over the responses made. Experimentation is important; much can be learnt even from failures. Often what is learnt in the process of working is of more value than the end product. Nevertheless, it is possible to produce successful work using the ideas and techniques described here.

DRAWING
TECHNIQUES

Finger drawing

Finger drawing and painting have a history dating back to primitive man. The earliest works of art in the Ice Age were lines drawn with fingers in damp clay, examples of which have been found at Altamira, in Spain.

A smooth, non-absorbent surface is needed, although finger drawings can be made on paper. Powder paint or liquid tempera colour mixed with cold water paste to a creamy consistency will serve well. There are two main processes: 1 *additive* − touching a finger (or other part of the hand) into the paint and drawing on the chosen surface; 2 *subtractive* − drawing with a finger into condensation on a window or into paint or printing ink on a formica, metal or glass tile. For the second method paint or printing ink can be poured or rolled onto the tile to produce an even surface cover. You should then draw into this with a finger, working quickly before the paint dries. A record of the drawing can be made by making a monoprint (see Printmaking − Monoprints, page 51). This is most suitable when the drawings have been made on a non-absorbent tile.

Free and spontaneous drawings can be made with this technique. In the hands of an artist such as Matisse, highly sophisticated drawings are achieved. It is a process which has much to offer all ages and talents in expressive work.

Pencil drawing

In the eighteenth century 'pencil' meant a brush, used in brushwork. While a medium hard pencil such as HB will answer most requirements, it is important to have experience of a wide range of pencils from 9B (very soft) to 9H (very hard). On occasion there may be uses for very soft pencils which tend to smear; and for very hard pencils which make light marks and impress the paper surface if any pressure is applied.

Coloured pencils are useful for colour notes when sketching, and can be used to produce high quality drawings, such as those by David Hockney.

Work based on free, spontaneous drawing will naturally lead to descriptive and narrative statements in creative expression. The quality of line or mark made is at least as important as what it may be used to represent − the artist's intentions are important.

Art gum or a kneaded eraser are most suitable for removing pencil marks. Rather than constantly rubbing out 'incorrect' or unwanted marks, use them to support future or consequent marks or lines. It is better not to be too hasty in erasing pencil statements. A 'Tortillon stump', used on pencil drawings will help produce subtle tonal transitions. A stump can be made with a tightly packed roll of cartridge paper (8 x 40 cm). Taper the end of the roll by gently sharpening it to a point with a craft knife. Use the point of the stump to rub down or over, or to draw into, soft pencil marks. A finger could be used instead of a paper stump, but it is less certain and requires care to avoid unwanted smears. 'Smudging' with the finger is more feasible where very soft effects are desired in large areas. Preferences will become evident after experience with the materials.

It is important to have experience of working on different kinds of papers, from wrapping paper and discarded envelopes to expensive hand-made papers, experimenting with smooth and rough surfaces, thick and thin, absorbent and hard surfaced papers. Good quality medium grain and medium to heavy grain drawing paper is suitable for most drawing instruments. It is as well to avoid shiny, gloss finished papers which are the least accommodating to pencil drawing. A high quality cartridge paper will not be less than 170 grammes per square metre (often written as g/m^2 in weight. For most work with pencil the weight of the paper should not be less than 95 g/m^2 (except for lightweight papers for notes and sketches).

Try to explore the creative possibilities of pencil drawing. Attention to visual aspects of the environment will be rewarding, especially when it leads to drawings of previously undiscovered factors. Try making pencil marks on different kinds of surfaces such as veneers, or a soft pencil on a sheet of metal foil which will result in an incised image. (see also Wet surface drawing, page 17 and Point Drawing, page 19).

Charcoal

Vine or willow charcoal is the best for general use. Synthetic and pencil form charcoal are made of carbon and both leave marks that cannot be as easily erased as those of vine charcoal. While charcoal has been increasingly used for drawing on white or tinted paper, its principal use is for making the preliminary drawings on walls or canvases as the first stage in a painting. A medium to rough surfaced paper is suitable for charcoal drawing.

Charcoal produces marks of varying tone, according to the amount of pressure used. It is unlikely to produce black, especially as it is apt to snap or to crumble with too much pressure. A matt, silvery grey is typical. The point or end of the stick of charcoal can be used, or it can be used along its length by drawing it flat across the paper surface. The use of charcoal is liable to lead to quick and superficial effects. It is useful for a 'free' technique on all kinds of papers – preliminary sketches for paintings, sculptures and so on, or for work demanding considerable control. It is advisable to use a fixative spray to prevent smudging. Experimentation can be rewarding; for example, try drawing with charcoal into wet oil colour on a board picture ground.

Corrections can be made in charcoal drawings by wiping with a damp cloth. Because corrections are easy to make, charcoal is ideal for sketches, particularly when working on a large scale. Other useful erasers are a plasticine rubber, putty, or new bread rolled or kneaded into a ball.

Try drawing with charcoal on sugar paper, pastel paper or on newsprint (kitchen paper).

Chalks

Working with chalk is in many ways similar to working with charcoal. It should be used in lengths of approximately 4 cm, both flat − to cover whole areas, and pointed − for line drawing. A preliminary outline is not necessary since it is an easy medium for stating masses and creating colour effects, either by movements outwards from a central mark or by moving the side of the chalk across the drawing surface.

Tonal effects can be varied according to the amount of pressure exerted. Care will be needed since chalks tend to crumble and snap under pressure. Colour mixing can be tried using a finger or a cloth to smudge or work the colours into each other. Only a limited degree of mixing in this way is possible; the surface of the paper may become eroded or broken.

Chalks work well on sugar paper or pastel papers. They can be used in combination with charcoal and pastels. Drawing on a highly textured ground is a worthwhile way of exploring the softness and subtlety of chalks. Chalks are versatile but they are not permanent − a fixative spray will be necessary to prevent smudging. Experiment with chalks in combination with other media to develop 'mixed media techniques'. The adhesive characteristics of other materials − such as liquid tempera colour or emulsion paint − can aid chalk adhesion to the picture surface. Use light chalks − white, yellow, orange − to draw highlights in a painting; or darker chalks for more detail. Chalk used in wet paint tends to blur. Try drawing with chalk on damp or wet paper. Much of the danger of the wet paper tearing can be obviated by resting it on a sheet of dry paper.

Experiment with different kinds, shapes and sizes of chalk, including natural chalk (it can be collected in a limestone area). All kinds of paper and card can be tried as drawing surfaces; try drawing also on wood, slate, wallpaper and fabric. Methods of working could include:

1   Dipping the chalk into a thin liquid paint or ink and drawing immediately on paper

2   Smudging chalk marks with a finger, soft cloth or cotton wool

3   Covering one side of a sheet of paper with chalk and drawing on the reverse side with a pencil or a ball point pen to transfer a chalk line to a second piece of paper under the chalk. This method

13

can be used to transfer to lino (for lino cuts) and to scraperboard when the chalk lines will need to be drawn over again with pencil before they are smudged

4   Making rubbings from textured surfaces (also Rubbings, page 44).

Pastels

Pastel consists of dry powdered colour mixed with gum (usually gum arabic) to bind it. Pastels can be blended over one another; finished work should be protected with fixative. The softest pastels give effects more related to painting, as in the work of Chardin; the hardest pastels (gritty in character) relate more to drawing. Degas tended to use the medium as a form of drawing rather than painting. He used black pastel on tinted paper for portaiture; and coloured pastels for his ballet studies. He experimented, manufacturing his own pastels and trying different techniques. For example he soaked his paper in turpentine before drawing — this helps to preserve the pastel drawing.

Try drawing with pastels on sugar paper, pastel paper or Ingres paper (which is more expensive) (see plate 5).

Crayons, wax and oil

It is advisable to decide on the range of colours to be used before drawing.

WAX CRAYONS   are well suited to large scale, free and expressive work and are also useful in sgraffito, rubbings and wax resist (see pages 41, 44, 42). Exploratory drawing with the crayons should prove rewarding. They can be used lengthwise — try drawing with a wax crayon after cutting notches along the side with a craft knife. Other possibilities include:

1   Painting over a wax crayon drawing with a brush dipped in turpentine or white spirit. The wax will tend to dissolve and the edges of colour areas tend to become less distinct.

2   Brushing a colour wash over a wax crayon drawing using water colours or inks to achieve interesting textured qualities. Further drawing can be superimposed, for example, by using pen and ink. Illusions of form can be created with this technique especially where highlights have been drawn in first using candle wax. Alternatively, decorative qualities can be suggested, as in John Piper's drawings and paintings.

3   Using a cheese grater to spread wax crayon over a sheet of sugar paper. Draw a design in the grated crayon with the wooden end of a paint brush, a stick or a finger. Cover the design with a clean sheet of drawing paper and press with a warm iron. Remove the

paper to see the transferred design.

4   Drawing with wax crayons the ends of which have been heated, for example, in a candle flame.

A number of manufacturers claim to market crayons that are unbreakable in normal use such as *Plastidecor*. Injection moulded in a polymer base compound, they do not melt in the hand; they can be sharpened with a pencil sharpener, and marks made can be rubbed out with a pencil eraser.

FABRICRAYONS   are wax crayons which hold a heat resistant dye suspended within them. They can be used freely on cartridge papers and transferred permanently to fabric by ironing. The colours are more intense on fabric than on paper. They only work on synthetic fabrics and should not be used on natural materials. The design, drawn on paper (for example, cartridge paper), is placed face down onto the fabric and heat applied. After ironing, the paper design is removed and the transfer is complete and permanent. The clearest results are obtained by cutting out the design before transferring it by ironing. Check the colour strength before removing the paper by carefully lifting a corner of the design. Further ironing should increase colour intensity. Washing does not affect the permanence of colours. The crayons can be used directly onto the fabric but less fabric wastage will occur if the design is first worked out on paper. They are clean to use. The technique can develop naturally from wax crayon drawings into fabric designs.

Of the synthetic fabrics, polyester is the easiest to colour with *Fabricrayons*. Other possible fabrics proceeding in order from the easiest to the most difficult to colour are: acrylic, triacetate, polyamides and diacetate.

OIL CRAYONS   have a soft consistency which is well suited to drawing animals and plants. They can be used for smooth and clear linear qualities, areas of colour or pulled lengthways across the surface to form textures and 'backgrounds'.

Oil crayons can be combined with felt tip pens, for example, when drawing on a large scale, for depth and density of tone and colour. The colours can be spread with ease and spontaneity. Their composition allows colour blending on the paper by rubbing one colour into another. Subtle colour mixtures are possible which, if necessary, can be changed by brushing turpentine over the surface. They are excellent for making quick 'on-the-spot' sketches for later translation into paintings. They can be used for sgraffito. As ordinary drawing crayons they need little 'fixing' as most are resistant to smudging. Should fixative be used, it does not detract from the colour brilliance.

Oil crayons can be used on most papers including sugar and cartridge papers. Experiment using them on different kinds of papers, including card and canvas paper.

AQUA-STICKS   which are water soluble crayons, are available from a number of manufacturing companies (eg Margros). The following ideas could be tried:

1   Draw with the crayons, then paint over the drawing using a brush and water

2   Touch the chosen crayon with a water laden brush and then draw on cartridge paper

3   Dip the crayons into water before drawing

4   Draw on damp or wet paper

While cartridge paper is suitable for all these experiments, they should be attempted on different kinds of surfaces. The colours can be mixed on the drawing surface whilst damp or wet.

Pen and ink

A wide range of nibs can be purchased for use with ink but it is worthwhile to experiment also with a variety of drawing instruments such as metal nibs of various shapes and widths; bird feather quills (try using the shaft and the feather); bamboo (shape the end); a twig; a stick or rod with one end split and a piece of sponge or felt inserted; a finger; and brushes. It is important to draw as directly as possible to preserve spontaneity. Pen and ink drawing is particularly suitable for stating the textural qualities of natural objects such as bark and shells.

Black and sepia inks are the most useful for drawing on white or light tinted papers. Cartridge paper (not less than 95 g/m^2) is appropriate but it is worth experimenting with different surfaces and colours of surface.

Pen drawing is suited to detail work, particularly against ink and water colour washes. Interesting effects are created by drawing on damp paper; lines will become blurred, 'feathering' may occur and the colour of the inks may mix.

Ballpoint pens

These can be used for drawing on all kinds of papers, but do not function well on greasy surfaces. They are useful for making quick sketches. Their soft, warm qualities are useful when sketching natural subjects such as portraits, trees and landscapes. It is difficult to gain much variation in the quality of line drawn. Depths of tone are best achieved by 'cross-hatching' (see Line drawings, page 18). It is possible to vary the thickness of the line drawn by exerting different amounts of pressure. (see also Wet surface drawing, page 17 and Point drawing page 19).

1 TONAL DRAWING: 'Study of the Transfiguration', Raphael (1483-1520). *Ashmolean Museum*, Oxford

2 IMPASTO: 'Woman Bathing' 1654, Rembrandt (1606-69).
National Gallery, London

3 BRUSH DRAWING: 'Titus' (original size), Rembrandt (1606-69).
British Museum, London

5   PASTEL DRAWING: Detail from 'Dancers on a Bench' 1898, Edgar Degas (1834-1917). *Glasgow Art Gallery and Museum*

LIMITED COLOUR RANGE (left): 'Don Quixote' c 1865, Honoré Daumier (1808-79). *Courtauld Institute of Art*, London

6 PENCIL AND WATERCOLOUR: Detail from 'Still Life' 1902-6,
Paul Cézanne (1839-1906). *Courtauld Institute of Art*, London

7 POINT AND LINE DRAWING: Detail from 'Wheatfield with
Cypress', Vincent van Gogh (1853-90). *National Museum Vincent van
Gogh*, Amsterdam

8   POINTILLISM: 'Young Woman with a Powder Puff' 1888-90,
Georges Seurat (1859-91). *Courtauld Institute of Art*, London

9 COLLAGE: 'Opened by Customs' 1937-38, Kurt Schwitters
(1887-1948). *The Tate Gallery*, London. Copyright Cosmopress,
Genève, and ADAGP, Paris, 1980

10   DECALCOMANIA: Detail from 'L'Europe après la pluie'
Max Ernst (1891-1976). *Wadsworth Atheneum*, Hartford, USA. The
Ella Gallup Sumner and Mary Catlin Sumner Collection. Copyright
SPADEM, Paris, 1980

11   WAX RESIST: 'Pale Shelter Scene', Henry Moore (1898-).
The Tate Gallery, London

12   ACTION PAINTING: Detail from 'Around the Blues' 1957-62,
Sam Francis (1923-). *The Tate Gallery*, London

13   PAINTING WITH A KNIFE: 'Forest' c 1959, Peter Coker (1926-).
Herbert Art Gallery, Coventry

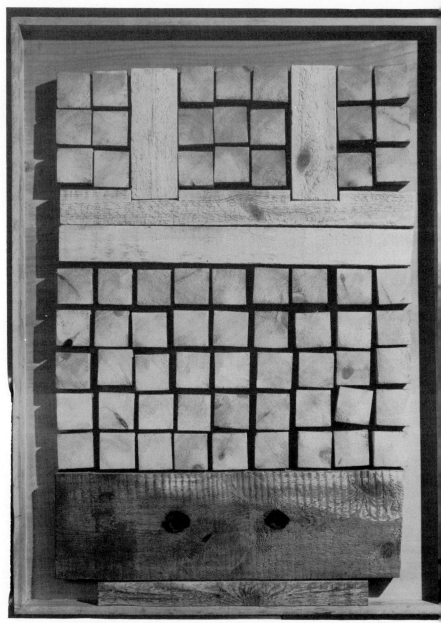

14   RELIEF — WOOD: 'Wood Relief' 1961, Joe Tilson (1928-).
The Tate Gallery, London

15 MOSAIC: Mexican Mosaic, 1953, José Chauvez Morado.
By courtest of the artist

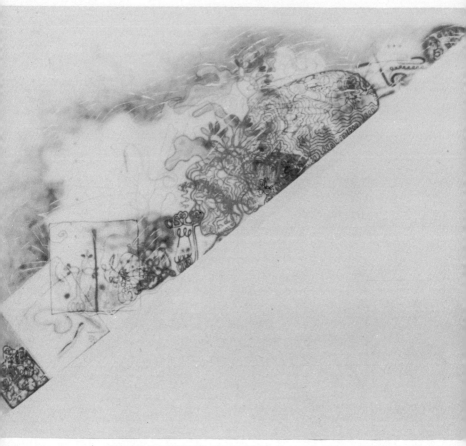

16 SPRAY PAINTING: 'Fall' 1964, Bernard Cohen (1933-). *The Tate Gallery*, London

Felt tip pens

These can be used for detail drawings or in a more spontaneous manner. They are most commonly used for statements of contrast, for example, drawing with a black pen on a white paper. Colour mixing is difficult to achieve with any consistency or certainty. The clarity of line possible makes these pens appropriate for working out ideas to be used for designs, for example, on fabrics. It is advisable to use the non-toxic felt tip pens.

The brilliance of colour and the wide range of colour choice makes these pens attractive. While they have a clear use for design work, patterns, sketches and poster work, they are limiting to colour exploration and the appreciation of tonal and linear variation unless used in combination with other drawing instruments. (see also Wet surface drawing below; Point drawing page 19; Techniques with inks – pen and wash drawing page 39; and Relief, miscellaneous and waste materials, page 65.) (See Techniques Using Inks – Drawing on wet paper page 38.)

Wet surface drawing

Marks made on wet paper with a pen and ink, or brush and paint, blur and separate to create interesting and often delicate effects. The images will be more difficult to control the more liquid or 'runny' the ink or paint. When the paper is dry further marks can be added to develop interpretations – a ball point pen, felt pens, pen and ink and coloured pencils could be used. All kinds of paper could be tried remembering that the thinner and lighter in weight the paper the more likely it is to tear when wet. Marks made on wet paper tend to leave an impression in the surface.

Brush drawing

Brush drawing has a tradition of calligraphic importance which includes Japanese and Chinese hieroglyphics, paintings on silk and brushed designs with pigments on pottery. Many artists make preliminary drawings with a brush on canvas or board before painting.

Working with a brush on paper or card can be rewarding; Most paints can be tried. It is worth taking the time to stretch the paper on a board (see Technical Notes page 89) if large areas of the paper are to be drawn on and if the medium is to be very thin liquid. Water based colours or inks work well on cartridge paper.

Areas of colour wash can be contrasted with more detailed brush work and drawings can be in a single tone or gradations of tone. Successive colour washes can be applied; a badger mop or large water colour brush facilitates the speed of application.

A variety of brushes should be tried on different surfaces. Good quality sable hair brushes are likely to offer greater subtlety and variety of usage. Different shapes of brush — round, filbert and chisel — will increase the repertoire. Try a range of brush sizes, for example, numbers 2, 6, 8, 12 (see also Point drawing page 19, and plate 3.).

Blown line drawing

Thinly mixed powder colours, thinned liquid tempera paint or inks will serve well. Use a brush or a drinking straw to transfer a few drops of colour onto a sheet of cartridge paper and draw them out across the paper by blowing through a straw held a short distance from the colour. The images produced can be interpreted and lines added using other drawing media such as pencils, pen and ink, felt tip pens and ball point pens. The images can be developed by superimposing blown lines of different colours. If the paper or card is tilted the drops of colour will run to produce linear progressions across the surface.

If clear definition is required each colour should be allowed to dry before subsequent colours are applied. Working wet-into-wet colours will produce unexpected and often exciting colour mixes, shapes and suggested textures, but is difficult to control.

Line drawing

An infinite variety of lines can be created. There is not space here to deal with all the very many ways of drawing lines. Experimentation is important, with new as well as traditional media. (Linear designs can also be created by cutting paper with scissors, with string and thread in collage work, engraving in wood and etching in zinc plate.)

Exploration could include the following ideas:

1 Continuous line drawing. Make a drawing in which the line drawn is unbroken. It might cross over itself but the maximum number of ends will be two. Draw the line (a) for its own sake; (b) as the stimulus for imaginative interpretations to be further drawn, painted or printed; or (c) as a representational drawing. Many variations are possible; and a choice of implements made from a wide range will be important.

2 Variations of tonal intensity by (a) pressure; (b) thickness or width of line; (c) variations in the spacing of lines will create different intensities; (d) cross-hatching — short strokes drawn over and in the opposite direction to patches of pencil lines made with the same drawing instrument. Line can be used to suggest volume; and a

greater sense of volume may be realised by cross-hatching to achieve the darkest tones and to suggest distance. The closer the lines the greater the intensity of tone. Attempts to state or suggest volume when drawing from objects that have been personally collected will be a worthwhile experience.

The other main uses of line drawing include the division of space, outline of shapes, creating a sense of texture and to communicate (for example, in calligraphy, cartography and cartoon drawings).

The following objects offer linear qualities to explore when drawing: dead plants and plants gone to seed; drift wood; creatures such as prawns, lobsters and insects; seaweed; trees in winter; fences and railings.

A line has a quality independent of what it represents in a drawing. Every line or mark has a vitality and dynamism of its own.

Point drawing

Drawings can be created with dots using different kinds of implements such as felt tip pens, ball point pens, pencils, paint brushes and prints and impressions from miscellaneous objects. Experimentation on different surfaces will be worthwhile. Attempts at designs with contrasts in the size, intensity, and the spacing of the dots can lead to exciting work. A large dot in a field of small dots (and vice versa) can become a focal point. The study of the 'Pointillist' technique used by Seurat (which he called Divisionism), Signac, Van Gogh and Picasso, and of the process of printing pictures in newspapers may prove a stimulus for future work.

If dots are to be made by printing from the ends of objects, for example, a twig, cork, or dowelling rod, a shallow tray or saucer will be required to hold the ink or paint. It is easier to control the colour if a sponge is placed into the saucer and the chosen implement pressed into the sponge until the required amount of colour is collected.

Felt tip pens on cartridge paper are suitable for this process. The continuous flow of ink is easily controlled and it dries quickly. There is a wide range of sizes of 'tip' to choose from.

It may well prove rewarding to study the theory of lines created from points (see Maurice de Sausmarez's *Basic Design*) and the combinations of point and line in the drawings by Van Gogh, Coldstream and Rembrandt. Joining dots or marks is an obvious example of this theory. It becomes particularly important in the work of Cézanne where dots and marks are placed at strategic points in a drawing, where they are dynamic and often centres of tension for forces of direction and form. (See plate 7.)

19

Tonal drawing

The technique of drawing indistinguishable transitions of tone was particularly important to the artists of the High Renaissance who developed Sfumato. Soft pencils, charcoal, chalks and pastels are suitable. The merging of shaded areas can be achieved by smudging with a finger (difficult to control particularly in small areas); use of an eraser (a dirty eraser can be used for dark tones); a piece of cloth or cotton wool. It is possible to work chalk, charcoal, conte crayon, and pastels into each other for subtle gradations of tone and colour. The choice of paper or card is important and you should test their suitability before use. A heavy duty paper is advisable if you intend rubbing across the surface.

For cross-hatching see Line drawing. The weight of the line can vary with the grade of pencil used and the pressure exerted in using it; and the width of the drawing implement will help to determine the width of the line or mark made. Variations in tone can be achieved by varying the density of pencil marks.

The study of light and shade is fascinating and it will prove valuable to study how it has been used by such artists as Raphael (plate 1) Caravaggio, Georges de la Tour and Correggio.

Off-set drawing

This can be attempted in a number of different ways. Try printing with the length of a piece of card, making each impression on the picture ground slightly to one side of the previous mark. This could also be tried with an old ruler, a roller, the end of a matchbox, or the side of the hand. Exciting rhythmic patterns can result, giving a sense of movement and of texture.

Progression through gradual transitions is the essence of off-set work particularly when concerned with tone, from light to dark or vice versa (see Tonal drawing, above).

Eraser drawing

An eraser can be used to make a drawing or in work using a combination of techniques. Cover a sheet of cartridge paper with soft pencil shading. Then use the eraser freehand or with the aid of geometric instruments (for example, against a straight edge or in a compass) to rub out areas. The size and shape of eraser will help determine the kind of mark made. Clean the eraser from time to time on a piece of scrap paper.

The removal of pencil marks or shading with an eraser is often a useful method for producing highlights in portrait drawing, figure drawing, still life and plant drawing. Exciting cloud and sea formations can be achieved in this way. Subtle changes of tone and of form can be realised. An eraser is useful for softening edges and for rubbing down or phasing out tone.

Textural drawing

Within the context of drawing we are concerned with the illusion of textural qualities, a surface division which can best be appreciated by sight rather than by touch. It is not always easy to isolate an area of texture, especially if it has been achieved by making 'rubbings' (see Rubbings page 44). Attention to detail can often lead to satisfying textural qualities of, for example, hair in portraiture, scales on a fish's back in a still life and grass or hedgerow in landscape. Pencils alone can be used to produce interesting textural effects. Experimentation is important in the selection of materials and in order to develop personal preferences.

It may be necessary to apply a general texture which is later worked over with the same media or mixed media. Areas could be masked out with a piece of card cut to shape. Textural drawing could be applied over a colour wash; or a wash painted over the drawing can produce interesting effects especially when the drawing is made with wax crayons (see Wax resist, page 42).

Combined drawing media

It is worthwhile exploring the possibilities of combining different drawing media in the same drawing. Suggestions can be found in many of the other sections of this book. The following could be tried and then used when required in future drawings: charcoal and chalk; pen and wash drawing; conte, chalks and pastels; pencils and charcoal; pencil or charcoal with wash (water colour or inks); wax crayon and water colour wash; and felt tip pen and colour wash. A combination of drawing media is particularly useful for rich textural qualities and for tonal gradations. (See plate 6.)

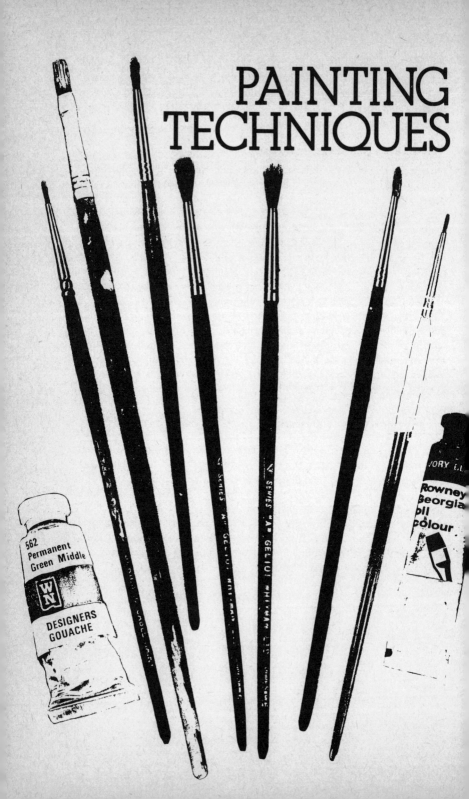

PAINTING TECHNIQUES

Finger painting

As well as being a technique for expressing sophisticated ideas by the most accomplished artists such as Klee, Dubuffet and Nolan, finger painting can be used when making 'roughs' for future paintings, and satisfies the needs of children to give immediate expression to individual experience and feelings. While the fingers and finger nails will do most of the work, especially when stating details, all the different parts of the hand and forearm are potential paint applicators.

The working surface should be non-absorbent so that the paint can be spread easily. Formica serves well, and either a formica topped table or an off-cut could be used. It is easy to wipe clean when it is not intended to keep a painting. A record of the painting can be kept by making a monoprint of it (see Printmaking – Monoprints, page 51). Other possible working surfaces include hardboard (first sealed with a coat of varnish, size or primer), perspex, cartridge paper (hot pressed is less absorbent than other varieties), sugar and hand-made papers and card. It is worthwhile stretching the paper (see Technical Notes page 89) on to a board before painting.

Possible painting media include powder colours or liquid tempera colours mixed with water and starch, cold water paste or polycell; and finger paint which can be purchased ready for use. Liquid tempera colours can be tried without starch. Oil colours give a richness of colour and are worth trying on primed hardboard, canvas board or stretched canvas (when only gentle finger pressure is advisable). Be sure to use a non-toxic paint. A spatula, spoon or a scrap of card will be useful to transfer the paint from its container to the painting surface. A 'bun tin' palette could be used to hold a little of the colours needed.

Very thin lines and details can be stated using a finger nail. Broader marks are more easily made using the palm of the hand, the heel of the thumb, the forearm or the elbow. The textures of skin and hair could also be involved. Experimenting with different ways of making marks in and with the paint will help develop an awareness of textural possibilities. Experiment will lead to a wider repertoire and, with thoughtful practice, to the development of a variety of skills. At first it is advisable to use one finger at a time. With experience, other parts of hands and arms can be incorporated. Similarly, it is advisable to use one colour at first, whilst skills are being developed. The colour range can be increased with experience.

Brush painting

See the Technical Notes page 74, for the choice of brushes available.

DRY BRUSH WORK

Use the paint thick, mixed with very little water. The brush strokes produced will be ragged, particularly on rough surfaced paper. This technique can be used to suggest the textures of, for example, bark, reeds, foliage, hair and building materials. Experiment with different kinds, shapes and sizes of brushes. Try using this method on damp paper.

WASHES
Mix enough water colour to cover the desired area. Hold the working surface (cartridge paper stretched on a drawing board) at an incline to allow the colour wash to flow slowly. Load the brush with colour and starting at the top left hand corner of the area to be painted, stroke the colour to the right reloading the brush as often as necessary. Reload the brush and start again at the left, touching the lower edge of the previous application of paint before it has dried, painting another band across to the right. It is important to keep the paint moist until the next layer or band of colour is applied. The process should be repeated for the whole of the chosen area. Any excess paint which collects at the bottom of the last application of paint can be removed before it has dried by drying the brush (on blotting paper or a rag) and using it to absorb the surplus paint.

STIPPLING
Use the brush loaded with colour and touch the paper repeatedly with it. Try using a variety of brushes to obtain interesting textures and a wide range of brush marks. This can be a useful way of stating atmosphere (as in the 'Pointillist' paintings plate 8), aerial perspective and suggestions of movement.

Painting with opaque colours
It is possible to paint over previous applications of colour when working with water colour mixed with white, poster colours, gouache and tempera colours. Whole areas can be reworked if required. Details and textures can be stated with comparative ease by overpainting. Try painting without first drawing with pencil or charcoal, to explore the potential of the colours.

The use of opaque colour is particularly important when working on a dark ground or over dark underpainting. Opaque colours have good covering properties and are particularly apt for design and poster work. They should be explored for their own characteristics in paintings. Opaque colours prevent light from reaching the picture ground. The light is reflected by the colours themselves and their true properties are more obvious to the eye. (Note that light penetrates transparent water colours, and is reflected by the colour of the picture ground, eg paper, which influences the paint colour as the light returns to the eye.)

Painting on a coloured ground

If transparent or translucent paints are being used, the colour of the paper can be used as a harmonising factor. Lighter shades of coloured paper are the most likely to be used. The more transparent the paints, the more the colour of the paper will influence the colour relationships in the painting.

Painting with a limited range of colour

A reduction in the number of colours to be used in a painting encourages the creation of colour variations and a greater awareness of colour properties and relationships. Many artists, such as Picasso and Braque in their early Cubist paintings, have used a limited range of colour; in many instances monocolour painting has been employed. This has often allowed concentration on other formal aspects of painting, such as structure and the relationships between shapes and facets of forms. A freer, more spontaneous use of monocolour painting can be seen in the work of Daumier (plate 4) and Delacroix.

Although it is usually thought more orderly to mix colours in or on a palette before painting, it is worth exploring the mixing of colours on the picture ground. The drier the paint mixture and the more absorbent the painting surface, the less time there is to do this before the paint dries.

Try painting a composition with one or two colours plus black and white. Colour harmony is most likely to result if colours are mixed. If your subject requires contrasts, a pair of complementary colours, such as red and green, should serve the purpose especially where they are placed in close juxtaposition.

Rag painting

The wide range of fabrics available gives scope for textural variations from the finest and most delicate marks with offcuts of nylon, rayon and silk, to the coarse, broader statements possible from using the rougher surfaced hessian. In between are many possibilities offered by natural fibres such as wool and cotton; man-made fibres, for example, polyester and dacron; and various combinations of both. Experiment with different fabrics so that you know which you will prefer for a particular piece of work.

Most fabrics can be used for large areas of a painting by making a ball or pad to be dipped into the paint for application to the picture ground. Cotton is a good all-round paint applicator. A piece of discarded cotton sheeting can be used for painting large areas and drawing with paint and is most suitable for painting details.

Rags are difficult to use for stating linear characteristics and the finest details (the corners and straight edges of sponges are more suitable for detail work). Nevertheless, if a rag is screwed-up or folded to leave pointed corners or jagged protuberances, clear and definite marks of detail can be achieved.The stiffer the fabric the more control can be exercised. Details can also be stated by wrapping a rag round a finger, and using the finger nail pushed tight against the fabric.

There are three main uses of rags for the artist:

1   Wiping away areas of wet paint (often valuable in printmaking particularly as a subtractive process in monoprinting) when the most suitable surface is primed hardboard especially when painting with oil colours.

2   As a textural contribution to a painting as in the work of Burri and Tapies. The fabric is made to adhere to the surface either with a suitable glue or dipped/mixed into the paint, such as emulsion paint, to give it thicker consistency.

3   To apply paint to a picture surface. For most purposes, painting with rags can be successfully done using water based medium on a hard-surfaced cartridge paper or card. A mixing palette is advised. Colour can be mixed with a palette knife on a formica tile (off-cut) or any non-porous surface (see Technical Notes pages 77, 85). A small plastic bowl will serve as a water container to dampen a rag before commencing work. A firm and stable working surface will be necessary. It is possible to complete a painting entirely with rags as applicators. Oil paints are considered to be the most satisfactory when working on a primed hardboard.

Try painting a landscape or a seascape where the rags will help to state clouds or turbulent seas, subtleties of tone, colour and movement.

Sponge painting

Sponges are commonly used in the studio for cleaning, creative print-making, and ceramics. They have been used by artists in combination with other techniques. Rarely have they been used alone for a painting. Yet it is possible to complete exciting and worthwhile work with a wide range of colours using only a sponge applicator. When paint is applied directly with a sponge, without reworking, the finished appearance is of spontaneity and a fresh surface quality. With experience, spontaneity can be combined with sensitive and subtle colour and texture.

Large areas can be painted, with little concern for detail, in a short space of time, by moving the sponge loaded with colour across the picture surface; repeatedly pressing the sponge directly on to the picture ground; or using a wiping action to remove areas of wet paint already applied. Precise detail is difficult to achieve with a sponge if working up to a line. It becomes easier where the sponge is used to make an area of colour or a mark creating its own sense of line.

NATURAL SPONGES   are more versatile and yielding to an artist's needs than synthetic sponges, but more expensive. Natural sponges are uneven in shape and difficult to cut to a precise shape. The smaller pieces are good for details and linear qualities. A fine mark (or line) can be made by pinching an edge between finger and thumb.

The quickest method of application is a wiping action across the picture ground. The less pressure used, the more 'streaky' the effect will be, since the paint will tend to be deposited by the sponge projections. With more pressure a better paint coverage is obtained.

SYNTHETIC SPONGES   are useful if you want to cover large areas with an even, flat coat of paint. Detail can be attempted using corners and edges or by cutting off small pieces. Any cross section shape or edge can be cut from the basic sponge forms using scissors. Try painting angles and linear structures such as buildings, scaffolding, bridges, street furniture (lampposts, bus stops, pillar boxes etc), and rock structures. Rounded sponges lend themselves to painting foliage, animals, clouds and sea.

Overpainting with sponge when using water based colours and exerting any degree of pressure tends to cause previous paint to be lifted by the sponge. This is particularly so if a slow wiping action is used.

There are many different shapes and sizes of sponge to try. Individual preferences will be clearer after experimentation. Working with a sponge that is moist will give a greater sense of control and probably more successful work.

STATING TEXTURAL QUALITIES WITH A SPONGE

The pore density of a sponge will influence the kind of mark made; the pore density is more pronounced the lighter the pressure used. A rigid working surface will allow you to exert pressure and use the sweeping movements which are part of the sponge technique. Ready mixed liquid or powder tempera colours are suitable for painting with sponges. A tray or palette will be needed for mixing colours before application. The opaque nature of gouache or poster colour lends itself to statements of detail which entails using a second or third colour over areas that have been painted with broad sweeps of the sponge. Examples include foliage in the foregrounds of landscapes, flower studies and textural statements in abstract paintings.

Sponges produce soft, mellow qualities when used with oils. Try working into the colour with a sponge while it is still wet so that the colour becomes much more a part of a primed board (or canvas).

It is possible to get a sense of achievement from working with only a sponge as an applicator of paint and inks, but it will have more use in combination with other methods of application. The full potential of sponges for painting has not yet been established. The imagery suggested by marks made with sponges can be developed using brushes, pen and inks, knives, rollers or whatever seems appropriate.

Paste engravings - combed pictures

This is a subtractive process in which images are created by engraving/ drawing into colour. Use a finger, stick, a comb cut from a piece of card (the teeth can be shaped differently from one comb to another), or an alternative implement to draw into paint mixed with cold water paste or starch that has been spread onto a tile, card or other working surface. Any of the paint mixtures and painting surfaces used for finger painting will work well.

Roller painting

Most of the usual painting media can be applied with a roller including oils, tempera and emulsion paint. Oils are particularly suited to working on a primed hardboard; emulsion paint can be used as an undercoat to oils as well as for painting. Tempera colour powder mixed with water can be used, but it is more difficult to achieve a uniform consistency than if using ready-mixed tempera colour in liquid or paste form.

Rollers (brayers) of various sizes will be needed. Highlights and smaller areas of detail are best achieved using a 4 cm roller and a 15 cm roller should be adequate for the large colour areas.

The greater the amount of pressure used when rolling colour across a surface, the more transparent the colour becomes. With less pressure, colour will be opaque but the area of colour will be broken. Colour quality can also be influenced by the quantity of paint used.

The hard, rubber-covered roller with a wooden core will give satisfactory results with most types of colour. A spongy roller is used to its best advantage with emulsion paint but even then it can too easily become too fully charged and produce a flat effect. Interesting areas of colour subtlety can be achieved; the roller is capable of producing translucent effects quite naturally.

The mixing and rolling out of colours (to ensure an even covering of the roller surface) is best done on a smooth, flat surface such as a formica tile. At times it may be desirable to have a separate palette for each colour.

Any firm surface, well supported, and reasonably smooth can be used for roller painting, such as hardboard — especially when using oil colours or emulsion paint; a sheet of card or cartridge paper — suitable when using a water-based medium such as tempera colour or block printing inks. Smooth surfaces allow a greater variety of effects for roller painting although roughened surfaces can give interesting results. Surfaces with deep depressions make painting with rollers difficult and are best avoided.

The use of rollers encourages the creation of broad vigorous marks, and can help to remove any inhibitions in the creative use of paint. It also prevents the painting from becoming too 'tight': it encourages the need to be concerned with the development of the painting overall, and not just a part at a time. If linear qualities are needed they can be achieved by: holding a roller at an angle so that only an end of it leaves a mark on the picture surface; or pressing the roller down once onto the picture surface and then lifting it to leave a line made along its length. Rollers are most suitable for stating spatial relationships which often occur when there is a strong sense of structure in a composition, for example, shapes to be found in built up areas. Human beings, animals, and plant life are more difficult to paint with rollers. It is probably better to leave portraiture until some experience has been gained with other subjects.

It is important to work logically from light to dark tones or vice versa. The first colour statements made with a roller should be areas of thin paint all over the picture surface. The large shapes can then be painted, after which many of the smaller shapes will fall into place. Layers of opaque colour painted over previous applications will bring the painting to a satisfactory conclusion. It is important to experiment with different kinds of paint, rollers and surfaces and with variations in technique in order to discover your personal preferences. The importance of practice and experiment for well thought out and prepared compositions cannot be overstressed.

Knife painting

The painting knife will perform certain effects that are very difficult to achieve with a brush. It is easier to produce a fine line with a painting knife, for example, when stating linear subjects such as sailing rigging, hair, wire and outlines of leaves and twigs. The knife enables purity of colour to be preserved even in the thicker areas of paint. Impasto painting (see page 35), typical of the painting knife technique, is attractive and often rich in colour. Working with a knife allows a direct, spontaneous approach often not achieved with the largest paint brushes. Interesting qualities can be created using the sgraffito process and by using the knife for scumbling.

29

TEXTURAL QUALITIES WITH A KNIFE

A wide variety of textural qualities can be created with a painting knife. Some of these include:

1   Scraping the knife loaded with paint over the picture surface. A grained ground such as canvas is particularly suitable. The white or colour of the grain will be exposed and seen against the colour of paint used which is held in the pores or recesses.

2   The sgraffito technique concerned with scraping away areas of wet or dry paint to reveal layers of colour previously applied or the colour of the picture ground. Highlights and contrasts of tone can be achieved in this way. A pen knife may prove more suitable for this process when the paint is dry. (See also Sgraffito, page 44).

3   Scumbling. Load the knife with colour and take it lightly across the surface, allowing the texture of the paper, board, canvas or the texture of the paint previously applied to catch the colour (see also page 35.)

4   Painting layer upon layer of colour to build rich textures. With the application of each layer, move the knife in the opposite direction to that previously made. This helps to knit the layers of paint together and a permanent picture surface is achieved. Plate 13 shows an example of knife painting by Peter Coker.

PAINTING DRAMATIC SUBJECTS WITH A KNIFE

Painting with a knife lends itself to dramatic subjects and to strong contrasts of light and dark, or to the use of complementary colours in juxtaposition. Tonal values are important, particularly when painting with a knife, because colour purity and intensity are much more in evidence. To achieve relative values of light and dark, the painting knife must be used in a direct and confident manner, moving it firmly across the picture ground. The subject matter should be understood before beginning to paint; if it is not, much paint will be wasted. A canvas surface will withstand a certain amount of pressure but a canvas board or primed hardboard are ideal for the dramatic treatment of subject matter. The painting knife lends itself to painting impasto (see Impasto page 35) and is therefore best used with oil colour.

PAINTING KNIVES WITH WATER COLOURS

Water-based tempera and poster colours can be used on sugar paper, cartridge paper and on card when painting with knives. Care is needed with fine pointed knives which may catch and break the surface of the paper or card. The absorbent nature of the painting surface makes working wet into wet difficult. The use of the knife with water-based media is not as yet established as part of the artist's repertoire and yet it has much to offer — an area to be explored. Perhaps the nearest a painting knife will get to a colour wash is when the surface of the paper is first dampened using a sponge. Then, with the loaded knife held horizontally, pull the 'flat' or back of the blade across the surface. Linear details are possible by holding the knife with the blade vertically above the paper. Allowing only the tip of the blade to touch the paper, move the knife across the surface, altering the direction for the desired effect. Liquid tempera colours are suited to this technique. Bolder directional marks can be applied by touching the surface of the paper with the tip of the knife in a horizontal position. Use gentle pressure to pull the knife across the paper. Broad areas such as sea, cloud formations, tree trunks and land masses can be applied with the full face of the blade. The paint is *pressed* onto the paper surface with the knife being lifted slowly away or moved across the surface as if spreading butter.

Spray painting

This is a technique which can be used to create diffuse atmospheres, tonal subtleties, interesting effects of colour mixing by spraying one colour over another in open layers of paint and to cover quickly a large area with an even coat of paint and a good degree of colour intensity. When used with masks, strong contrasts of shape, tone and colour can be made. (See Technical Notes, page 87 for a description of the type of equipment needed for spray painting.)

SPRAY PAINTING WITH MASKS
Masks facilitate sharp contrasts between clean cut shapes and diffuse areas of colour. It is essential to mask off all areas of a painting that are not intended to receive paint. The most usual ways are by using masking tape, sellotape, templates cut from card to mask particular shapes, miscellaneous objects (for example, pieces of fabric, machinery, wood and stones), shapes torn or cut from paper, and 'fixing' materials such as rubber cement. Various arrangements of the mask(s) could be tried with subsequent applications of paint in different colours. Masks should be left in position until the paint has dried. It is better to give two light sprayings, one over the other after the first application has dried, rather than one heavy or full spraying when colour flooding or pools may occur.

Spray painting is still a relatively unexplored activity in creative work. It has recently gained popularity in custom painting to decorate motorized vehicles. Its use in picture and design making by artists such as Bernard Cohen and Ian Stephenson developed mainly in the 1960s. There is room for experiment and exploration. Try using spray paint to achieve textural harmonies and for precise, detailed work, as well as in the ways in which they are more usually employed. (See Techniques with Inks — Sprayed pictures, page 39, and plate 16.)

Action painting

The surface of an action painting with its swirls, dots, wrinkles and encrustations of colour can become a rich tactile experience. The sense of 'wanting to touch' can be enhanced by the use of additives. As well as applying paint with different tools such as sticks, trowels, knives, try mixing a heavy impasto (see page 35) with powder colours, sand, Polycell, broken glass (in school try using small pieces of shattered car windscreen, which are less dangerous) or other foreign matter. Hardboard will accommodate and hold many different kinds of paint and other media and is eminently suitable for action painting whether primed or not. (See the Technical Notes page 83 for other action painting surfaces).

Suggestions for applying the paint include dripping, flicking, throwing (try a sponge loaded with colour), pouring, blowing, spreading (use fingers and hands, a spatula or knife) and pressing (see Decalcomania).

Try action painting to music. Different aspects of the music may be emphasised in each piece of work. The most obvious may be the rhythm when the action of the painter will be influenced by the pulse of the music.

It is advisable to try each of the suggestions separately at first to gain knowledge of some of the possibilities and individual preferences. Then different combinations of them could be tried in successive paintings. There is an exciting world to be explored here and it will be important to share experiences. Children should be allowed to make their own discoveries as well as try the ideas given here.

Decalcomania

A method first used by the surrealist painter Oscar Dominguez and adopted by Max Ernst (for example in his 'L'Europe après la pluie' — plate 10). It is a process of squashing areas of wet paint on the canvas, board, card or paper. Try the following:

1 Making a symmetrical pattern by blotting. Drip or splash paint onto one half of a sheet of paper. Fold the other half of the paper over it and give light pressure. When opened out the paint will have formed a symmetrical shape which can be worked on or kept for its own qualities.

2 'Tonking' — a method which Professor Tonks suggested to his students in the early years of this century. Lay a piece of waxed or greaseproof paper over paint while it is still wet. Apply light

hand pressure then pull the paper away. Interesting textural effects will result, with the paint pulled up into projections. This method is most effective with oil colours or with thicker consistencies of poster, powder, tempera paste and liquid tempera colours. It could be tried when a painting is partially complete or to influence the whole of the finished surface.

3 Pressing certain areas of a painting. This is most easily effected when the areas to be pressed are appreciably thicker than the remaining parts of the painting. Paper, card, perspex, glass and fabric can be tried. Certain materials can be cut to cover only the shape of the area to be pressed. The impression made on the sheet material used for pressing is worth keeping for consideration for future work. It can either be used as the basis for interpretations to be made, appreciated for its own qualities or used in collage.

4 Press a sheet of newsprint or cartridge paper over colour that has been rolled out on a tile or palette. Designs could be developed on either the print taken or the colour left on the tile. Variations on this include dampening the paint or ink so that the colour becomes more fluent and takes up interesting shapes, textures and colour mixtures. Try pressing with different grades of papers and cards. It is advisable to pull the two surfaces apart soon after contact; they may be difficult to separate if left for a time.

Additives

The line dividing painting and sculpture is thin and, at times, a broken one. Painters have projected their picture surfaces into relief. The Cubists, for example, when concerned with collage techniques, introduced onto the picture surface everyday materials such as newspaper, cloth and cardboard. Kurt Schwitters carried this further, including in his compositions objects that might normally be considered as waste, such as bus tickets. Paul Klee experimented with glue and plaster to form a ground on which he painted with brilliant colour. Dubuffet used oil paint with additives such as sand and coal dust. Robert Rauschenberg has built out surfaces into relief, integrating screen printing techniques with the use of waste materials. The term 'matter painting' is often used to describe paintings which involve thick and varied media.

It would be sensible to begin with the accessible, ready to hand materials:

DRY POWDER COLOUR   can be sprinkled onto wet paint or a pva binder. The granules of powder will contribute to rich and interesting surfaces.

SAND   varies in texture from coarse to fine, and is found in colours

33

such as yellow, brown, grey and white. It can be used:

1   To enrich the textural possibilities of painting media. Mix the
    sand with the chosen powder or liquid tempera colour (add a
    little pva binder to increase adhesion); emulsion and oil colours
    could be tried. The mixing can be done with a palette knife or a
    plasterer's trowel on a mixing palette. Since the paint will now be
    thick and heavy, it is advisable to work on a firm ground such as
    card or board (thinner consistencies could be tried on cartridge
    paper). The paint/sand mixture is best applied with a spreading
    action.

2   In the technique Marmotinto. Sprinkle natural sand over a drawing
    that has been made with an adhesive (a pva binder is advised) on
    paper or card while the binder is still wet. The composition can be
    developed with paints, pastels, crayons or felt tip pens.

Sand painting is similar except that the sand is coloured prior to use
with inks, or mixed with paints. Once the sand has been sprinkled over
the adhesive, shake or pour off the excess sand into a suitable container.
Sand that remains held by the adhesive will take up the directions of
the drawing. Subsequent applications with different colours can be
made once the adhesive has dried.

STARCH   can be mixed with colour: the more starch used in the
mixture, the lighter the shade and more opaque the colour will be. It is
advisable to use the mixture on a strong inflexible surface such as hardboard or a thick card. On a flexible surface the colour will tend to crack.
This can be obviated by mixing a few drops of gum arabic with it. The
marks peculiar to certain applicators will remain when using colour
mixed with starch.

SOAP   comes in two main forms:
    (a) block – load the applicator with colour before touching the soap
with a rubbing motion; (b) liquid – mix the chosen colour with water
then pour a little soap into it, six parts colour to one part soap. To
make 'bubble pictures' or designs, place a little of the liquid soap
mixture into a beaker or jar. With a drinking straw held in the mixture
so that one end is just below the surface, blow into the liquid until
bubbles rise over the lip of the beaker. Remove the straw and place a
clean sheet of paper (cartridge or newsprint) over it to take an
impression from the bubbles. This can be repeated as often as is
necessary to produce a satisfactory design which can be kept for its
own qualities or developed with other media such as pen and ink.
    The addition of soap can help to control the painting of water
colour washes ,as it will soften the colour values. A good method is to
mix the required colour first and load the chosen applicator with it
before touching the soap for mixing. The mixture will not spread as
easily as pure, water-based media. Since soap has adhesive properties

it is difficult to remove colour that is mixed with it.

COOKING OIL   mixed with tempera colours will provide a smoother consistency which can be painted onto sugar paper, card or board. It provides a different, interesting textural quality.

There are many other substances to be tried as paint additives. Flour, cold water paste, saw dust and wood shavings are but a few of the possibilities that are readily available.

Glazing

Glazing is the application of successive layers of transparent or translucent colour, usually applied when the first colour has dried. The lighter and more resilient the colour of the underpainting the more effective it will be. The darkest layers of colour are the last to be applied. The result is usually of a more luminous colour especially when using oil paints. Titian obtained depth and glow of colour with this method. More recently a similar technique has been employed by David Hockney working with acrylics on canvas.

Scumbling

Scumbling is a useful method of stating impressions of foliage, clouds, certain effects of water and painting highlights such as those often to be seen on foreheads, noses, knuckles of the hand and crests of waves. It can be used to create interesting textures for their own qualities.

The easiest method is that used when painting with a knife. Load the knife with colour and take it lightly across the surface allowing the texture of the paper, board, canvas or the texture of the paint previously applied to catch the colour. If this process is being used to state highlights it will involve painting light over darker tones. The opaque nature of oil colours and, to a lesser degree, of poster paints, makes them most suitable for scumbling techniques. Powder colour and liquid tempera colour could also be tried with a knife or a brush.

Impasto

This is concerned with the application of thick paint, often used towards the end of a painting process to state certain details and highlights. A fine example of this can be seen in Rembrandt's 'Woman Bathing' (plate 2). In oil painting it refers to the physical substance of the pigment particularly when heavy enough to be raised above the surface, catching the light and throwing a slight shadow of its own and so adding to the liveliness as well as solidity of effect. It is often heavily

35

loaded in the light areas, only the shadows being left transparent. Some painters such as Van Gogh have used impasto with uniform emphasis. A strong card, hardboard or a stretched canvas, with care, could be used as the picture ground.

TECHNIQUES
USING
INKS

Drawing on wet paper

(see Drawing Techniques — wet-surface drawing page 17). Use a brush or pen to draw with ink on wet paper. Wet the paper on both sides before placing it onto a wet drawing board — or a formica topped table. Sponge or wipe away excess water. Draw quickly over the damp surface. The paper can be redampened with a wet sponge. Waterproof inks once dry cannot be affected by adding more water. Felt tip pens can be touched to damp paper (try working on blotting paper) when the colours will spread and separate into their constituent tints.

POWDERED INK ON WET PAPER

Deposit powdered ink onto wet paper by flicking, dropping or sprinkling. Subtle colour relationships can be achieved, and, when dry, interpretations and additions made using brush and pen and ink.

Gouache and ink

To create alternating designs of black and white, paint all the areas that are to be white (which can be drawn first with pencil if desired) with water soluble, thick, white gouache or poster paint. A little colour could be mixed with the white paint to distinguish it from the white paper. When the paint is dry, cover the whole composition with a coat of black indian ink; leave it to dry. Then wash the paper under a gently flowing cold water tap. Use a sponge carefully to wipe the paint off the paper. The ink will remain in place except where it is painted over the white paint. When the paper is dry, additional work can be added with black or coloured inks.

It is important to test and experiment with equipment. Some gouache colours will not lift off the paper easily where manufacturers have given them an emulsified base.

Brush and wash drawings

These are usually made on cartridge paper with coloured inks, but water colours could be tried. The ink can be diluted with water which makes it suitable for monotone work, depending on the variations of tone of the chosen colour. A good quality sable hair brush is best but satisfactory results can be achieved using cheaper squirrel hair or ox hair brushes. A hog hair brush may be useful for variations in texture. Try using a range of brushes for varying widths of line and types of mark. It is worthwhile stretching the paper first to prevent it warping (see Technical Notes page 89).

Pen and ink details could be added to complete the work if necessary. (See Drawing Techniques — Pen and ink page 16, Brush page 17 and Painting Techniques — Washes page 24).

Pen and wash drawings

A metal nib or fountain pen with ink will create interesting contrasts of fine line to tonal areas stated by washes with the brush. This can be particularly useful for plant studies, stating drapery and in portraiture. Ballpoint pens could be incorporated and felt pens used when colour washes are dry. Pen and brush with ink and colour washes work well on cartridge paper that has been stretched on a board (see Drawing Techniques – Pen and ink **page** 16 and Painting Techniques – Washes page 24).

Blot pictures

Put some drops of coloured ink on one half of a sheet of paper. Fold the other half over and press. Unfold to reveal a symmetrical image which could be interpreted by additions with drawing or painting media.

Try making a drawing or painting with ink and brush on one half of the paper; proceed as above. Unfold the paper to see a transferred image. Subsequent drawings can be made on top of the first to create exciting imagery. (see Painting Techniques – Decalcomania page 32).

Sprayed pictures

Spray techniques can be used in combination with other methods of making marks with inks. It is usual practice to use a card or paper template to mask or cover areas not to receive sprayed colour. It is advisable to use several light layers of spray to build up the intensity of colour needed. The work should be allowed to dry before removing the mask. Pen and ink lines can then be added for details in areas that were previously masked, or over the colour sprayed onto the picture surface.

While a mouth diffuser will suffice, a spray gun with an adjustable nozzle is advisable. It is essential to wash diffusers and spray nozzles with warm soapy water and then to rinse with clear water, to remove ink residue. (See Painting Techniques – Spray painting page 31).

Combined media using ink

Inks can be used with a variety of media. Possibilities include:- wax resist, sgraffito with water colours, powder and liquid tempera colours, gouache and poster colours. Experiment with different techniques to develop your personal preferences. Many of the processes can be found under separate headings in this book. For blown techniques using pen and ink see Drawing Techniques – Blown line, page 18.

SGRAFFITO AND ENGRAVING PROCESSES

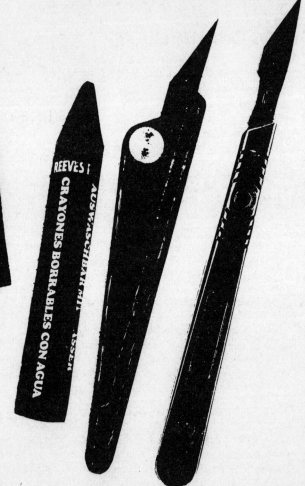

Wax engraving or sgraffito

Cover a sheet of cartridge paper (sugar paper or card could be used) with wax crayon. Either a design or a composition can be made as long as most of the paper is covered. Paint over the crayon with black ink or black powder colour mixed with detergent, or cover the design with black wax crayon. Use a pointed instrument such as a cocktail stick, lino-cutting tool or point of a pair of scissors to make a drawing by scratching away the black cover to reveal the colours beneath.

SGRAFFITO USING COLOURED PAPERS
Working on white paper will give a clear image when seen in contrast to black or dark colours. However, a coloured paper revealed when black paint or black ink is scraped away can produce subtle colour relationships and increased colour harmony (as opposed to colours neutralised by white).

Scraperboard

Scraperboard is a refined pipe clay which has been rolled under pressure while damp into a sheet of strong white paper and lightly sprayed with black waterproof indian ink. It must be throughly dry before it is used. Scraperboard can be purchased ready for use with a black surface or a white surface to which ink can be added. A drawing is created by scratching through the ink with a sharp instrument — a scraper board tool, lino tool or a craft knife. The white surfaced board offers a wider range of creative possibilities since coloured inks could be used instead of black. The ink must be dry before commencing work. With practice, highly sophisticated designs can be created. It is important to practise with the different scraper tools to gain control and knowledge.

Should a preliminary drawing be made it can be transferred to the scraperboard by covering the reverse of the drawing with white chalk and then carefully placing it over a piece of scraperboard cut to the size of the drawing. Hold the paper in place (use paper clips) while drawing over the design again to transfer white chalk lines onto the black scraperboard. Remove the paper and before the chalk lines can smudge draw over them with a pencil.

Scraperfoil

Scraperfoil consists of sheets of aluminium surfaced boards which have been given a matt black coating. It can be worked in the same way as scraperboard.

Plaster engravings

Pour plaster into the bottom of a cardboard box or lid to a depth of 3-5 cm. (see Technical Notes, page 85, for details on mixing plaster). When the plaster has set, paint it with a dark colour (poster colours or inks). Use a pointed instrument to scratch a design to reveal the white plaster through the colour. George Braque used this technique on large plaster slabs coated with black paint and produced designs of incised mythological deities. They are inspired by Greek and Etruscan bronze mirrors.

A print could be taken from an incised block of plaster by 'inking' it using a roller and carefully placing a sheet of white paper over it. Hand pressure (or a clean roller) on the paper should be sufficient to complete the print. Remove the paper from the block of plaster and leave it in a suitable place to dry.

Encaustic painting

Hot wax painting is a process which uses powdered colour added to molten beeswax and then applied to the picture ground, a primed board or canvas, with a brush or knife. The beeswax can be mixed with the powder colour in an enamel plate or a tin lid which has to be warm to keep the wax malleable. Alternatives include candle wax and wax crayons. Melt the wax crayons (having first removed the paper wrappers) and drip the coloured wax onto a sheet of sugar paper. Since the work will have to be done at some speed it is advisable to make a plan or drawing and to touch the heated crayons onto the paper. This process can take a long time to complete, as once removed from the warm receptacle the crayons solidify very quickly. At first, work done is likely to be experimental.

Although a wax emulsion has been used in some modern wall paintings, this is distinct from the 'burning in' process which the word encaustic implies.

Wax resist

Draw with a candle or wax crayons of a light colour on cartridge or sugar paper. Brush a darker coloured (or black) ink or water colours over the drawing so that it remains on the undrawn parts of the paper but is resisted by the wax. This is a technique employed by many artists, including Henry Moore in his war time shelter drawings and John Piper in his water colours and many sketches. It provides the possibility of creating rich textural qualities with comparative ease. Overlays of colours can be tried and subsequent applications of wax drawn over the colour washes when they are dry. (See plate 11.)

RUBBINGS AND FROTTAGE

A wide range of media can be used including heel ball, wax crayons, conte crayon, pastels and chalk. It is worthwhile considering the rubbings and frottage of Max Ernst, who used a range of media from pencil to oil colour. These were applied to the canvas, then, with the canvas stretched tight over an interesting texture, the oil colour was scraped hard across the surface of the canvas using a knife.

The simplest method of taking a rubbing is by placing a sheet of newsprint over the chosen surface and rubbing over the paper with a thick wax crayon. The principle of rubbing can be simply understood by placing a small sheet of newsprint over a coin and rubbing with a pencil or crayon. A specialized form is that of brass rubbing for which permission must be sought from the local clergy. Many churches have medieval brass plate monuments inlaid in the floor. But there are so many interesting surfaces around us that much worthwhile creative work can be done in the everyday environment.

Choose a wax crayon which will give a strong contrast to the white or colour of the paper to be used; newsprint is suitable. Lay the sheet of paper over the chosen texture and holding it steady (it could be taped down at the corners) use the whole length of the wax crayon to make the rubbing. Certain parts can be given emphasis by exerting greater pressure.

Frottage

Look at the rubbings made to see if they suggest interpretations that can be made. The frottage is completed by collecting suitable rubbings from different surfaces, on the same piece of paper in the process of completing a drawing. This is more complex than taking a rubbing from a single surface or single object.

Rubbings from natural objects

Possibilities include wood grain, leaves, shells, bark, certain weeds and seaweed. Each can be used as a single motif, or in combination and the rubbings enjoyed for their inherent qualities, or as starting points for interpretations.

Rubbings from man-made objects

Such objects usually offer more angular, mechanical shapes. The following could be tried: wire mesh, grids, scissors, brickwork, keyholes and polystyrene. Care will be needed not to tear the paper on metal corners and projections. Interesting rubbings may be gained from textured wallpapers and glasspapers.

Textures created in art work

The textures of paintings, collages, sgraffito and wax resist, embroidery and appliqué work could be used. The surfaces of sculptures will provide interesting rubbings, for example, those carved from brize blocks, plasticell, plaster of Paris, chalk and soap.

Collages from rubbings

Use rubbings to create collage designs on a card or sugar paper base. Cut or tear the rubbings to the shapes required. Arrange them on to the base and fix into position with a pva binder. Only a small amount of adhesive is needed, touched along the edges of the paper shapes. Rubbings in different colours will allow the development of colour relationships in the collage work.

Rubbings superimposed and combined with other media

Superimposition can give a sense of movement; or can be used to build up tonal areas. Slightly off set subsequent rubbings from the same textural shape, one from another.

Combined with other media, such as colour washes, pencil drawing and printing techniques, compositions can be completed which have a richness and variety of textural and colour qualities. Alterations can be made during the process of working by placing rubbings as collage over unwanted drawn lines and colour areas, and *vice versa*.

PRINTMAKING

Relief Printing

VEGETABLES

Cut a motif from the cross-section or the end of a potato leaving the intended form to appear in relief. Poster colour or liquid tempera colour is then applied (with a brush or by pressing the potato onto a sponge pad which is lying in the colour mixture in a shallow dish or saucer; see Stick prints, below). Press the potato motif onto a sheet of paper (cartridge paper or newsprint) to take a print. With repeat printing, changes in colour and combinations of different motifs, interesting decorative work can be achieved. The print can be made waterproof by mixing a little pva binder with tempera colours before printing or by applying a coat of beeswax over the finished work.

STICK PRINTS

A similar process to that used with vegetables. Care will be needed with knives (craft knife or hack saw) used to cut a motif in relief at the end of the stick; a vice would be helpful. Try using balsa wood or dowelling rod. Often sticks and lathes have interesting end textures that are worth printing without recourse to cutting implements. The end of any stick like object can be used. Normally the stick will need recharging with colour after every three or four prints. Make test prints to see how thick the paint or printing ink should be and how much is required. Stick prints are particularly useful for more intricate designs than can usually be achieved with vegetables. To charge the motif with colour, press it onto a sponge pad — place a piece of sponge or foam plastic in a tray, saucer or tin lid; soak the pad with ink, ready mixed tempera colour or dye.

CARD EDGE PRINTS

Printing with the edge of different widths and lengths of card is an interesting method of image and picture making, both representational and abstract. Smaller pieces of card can be charged with colour by pressing onto a sponge pad (see Stick prints). Colour can be brushed onto longer lengths. Absorbent cards will necessitate speed of printing before the colour dries (See Drawing Techniques — Off set drawings, page 20).

STRING PRINTS

Dip the string into powder colour or liquid tempera colour and place it onto one side of a sheet of newsprint (or kitchen paper). Fold the other half of the paper over the string and take a print applying hand pressure.

Interesting variations can be created by leaving one end of the string exposed from the paper. Place a drawing board on top of the paper and, holding the paper steady, pull the string out from the paper. Try pulling in different directions with subsequent prints to explore possibilities. The images created can be kept or developed further with drawn, printed or painted marks.

String can be arranged into a design and stuck (use a pva binder) into position on a block or rectangular base – see Waste blocks page 49 – and then printed. A stronger paper such as sugar or cartridge paper should be used if much additional work is to be done.

STRING PRINT WITH A CYLINDER

Arrange the string tightly around a cardboard cylinder; hold it in position with a pin at each end whilst fixing it to the cylinder with a pva binder. Alternatively, brush the pva adhesive over the cylinder before pulling the string into place round it. When the adhesive is dry, colour can be applied with a brush, or by using a tile. Spread an even consistency of water-based printing colour over a formica tile with a roller, then roll the cylinder along the tile to charge it with colour. With gentle hand pressure, roll the cylinder over the chosen paper surface to take a print. The cylinder can be rolled in different directions across the paper.

CRUMPLED PAPER

Crumple a piece of paper so that it can be held comfortably in the hand. Print from the crinkles in the paper. Apply colour to the paper by pressing it onto a sponge in a saucer of colour (see Stick prints page 47). Print on newsprint or cartridge paper.

WOOD GRAIN

Use a roller to apply the colour to the chosen wood grain, or paint it on with a brush. An even consistency and covering of colour should be looked for. A satisfactory print can be obtained by placing a sheet of newsprint over the wood and applying hand pressure or using a clean roller. The prints can be repeated to produce a design. Other objects could be introduced to print from in the one design.

PAPER PRINT

Arrange and stick cut and/or torn paper shapes to a card base. Roll ink (see Cut card print page 49) over the surface and take a print. Whereas it is usual to work with paper of the same thickness, you could also try using differently textured papers in the same design.

PRINTING FROM PVA ADHESIVE

Paint a design with the pva binder on paper or card. When dry, use a roller to apply colour to the surface. Place a clean sheet of newsprint or cartridge paper over it and take a print – hand pressure should suffice.

CUT CARD PRINT

Use a roller to apply colour to a shape cut from card or paper (use old newspapers to protect work surfaces). To ensure an even consistency of colour on the roller, first roll out the colour on a tile — formica or glass. Place the cut shape, colour upward, onto another piece of paper. Carefully lay a sheet of newsprint or cartridge paper over it and take a print using pressure from a clean roller.

MISCELLANEOUS OBJECTS

Assorted objects found about the house or garden are an endless source of inspiration for creative printmaking. The possibilities include driftwood, polystyrene, leaves, cork, wire mesh, vegetable net bags, cotton reels, bark, buttons and twigs. Those which can be laid flat could be used in a waste block print. Individual items can be hand-held (eg a cotton reel) or mounted on a small wood block (off-cut), for example when printing from a button or milk bottle top. Leaves and more fragile objects are best printed by first applying printing ink to the surface using a roller before placing onto a clean sheet of paper — ink upwards. Place a second sheet over the top to take a print — hand pressure will usually be sufficient. A soft rag is useful as a pad for exerting pressure in corners or where a projection proves a barrier to less prominent parts. Repeated prints from the same object or in combination with marks printed from a variety of objects will help to create exciting images and designs.

WASTE BLOCK PRINTING

This technique is sometimes known as collage print since it is an impression taken from the surface of various materials which have first been arranged then fixed down upon a card or board base before 'inking-up'. The materials used may come from many sources. Any surface, to which it is possible to apply colour with a roller, (see Cut card print) and which is firm enough for an impression to be taken from it, could be used. The waste materials should be chosen for their textural qualities. The particular qualities of one material become more evident when placed in contrast to other materials. The arrangement of the materials into a design or pictorial composition will contribute to the success of the print and it is worth spending some time exploring ideas before finally fixing materials in position.

PLASTICENE

Try printing from a block of plasticene. Make impressions into a side or end of the block using, for example, a cocktail stick or a pencil. Attempt to organise the marks made into a design. The surface can be rolled with printing ink (see Cut card print), and a print taken by pressing the block onto a sheet of paper. Too much pressure may result in the form of the block becoming distorted.

A single motif, pressed into the end of a block of plasticene, could be used as a stamp. It will not be possible to print many editions from one block since the plasticene will gradually change shape with pressure. As much as this may be regarded as a disadvantage, it could be explored for the changing imagery in subsequent prints. Load the motif with colour using a sponge pad (see stick prints, page 47).

WOOD BLOCKS
Wood has been the principal material used for producing relief blocks. Wood cuts are made in the block with a knife and variously shaped gouges on the plank or grain side of softer woods such as maple, cherry and pear. Wood engravings are made from the end or cross grain surface of harder woods such as holly and box. Wood blocks are expensive and it is therefore sensible to work with alternative cheaper materials, for example, lino, to gain the necessary skill in handling the various tools.

LINO PRINTS
Off-cuts from ordinary floor linoleum can be used. Practise with lino cutting tools by cutting direct designs based on the natural shapes made by the tools. Keep the hand holding the lino steady behind the cutting tool. Water-based inks are cleaner to use but oil-based colours give more subtlety and richness of colour.

ONE COLOUR PRINT   Use lino cutting tools to cut a design in the lino surface. Parts cut away will appear the colour of the printing paper (usually white). Ensure that all the lino chippings have been removed before using a roller to apply an even consistency of printing ink (see Cut card prints, page 49). Place a sheet of newsprint or cartridge paper over the design and use a clean roller to apply pressure over the back of the paper. Carefully pull the paper away from the lino to complete the print. Try printing on different kinds and colours of papers.

MULTI-COLOUR, SINGLE BLOCK PROCESS   sometimes known as waste or reduction lino cutting. Cut out parts of the lino which are required to preserve the colour of the printing paper. Print as many editions as are required before proceeding – these could all be one colour or each one a different colour. Clean the lino with a damp rag. Having printed the first colour(s), cut away more of the lino. Print the second colour on top of the first colour. Make sure that the lino is in alignment with the first print so that the areas cut away in the second cutting will leave the first colour visible. Continue the process for subsequent over printing until the multi-colour print is complete (or the lino entirely reduced). Interesting colour and textural qualities can result from allowing some areas of the first colour to be overprinted with subsequent colour applications.

MULTI-COLOUR, MULTI-BLOCK PROCESS   It is advisable to make a preliminary drawing. Decide the number of colours to be printed in order to determine the number of lino blocks required. Make a tracing from the drawing of the first colour area to be printed – usually the colour which gives the clearest reference to the overall design. Trace the design onto the lino block, having first reversed it so that it will print the correct way round. Use the 'v' shaped lino cutting tool to cut round the shapes where a firm boundary to the colour is required. Gouges should be used to remove areas that are not to be printed. When the lino is ready for printing, use a roller to apply an even consistency of printing ink to the surface (see Cut card print, page 49). If a registration frame is used, the printing paper should be cut to size allowing for at least a 5 cm margin all round the lino block. Alternatively, draw a frame round the lino block with a pencil on a sheet of paper, which will act as the guide or base. Place the lino block into position within its frame. Place printing paper down onto the inked block so that it registers exactly with the base sheet. With a clean roller apply pressure over the back of the paper to take a print. Lift the paper at each corner to ensure that a good impression has been made before completely removing the paper. Make the required number of prints from this key block. Proceed to take impressions from the second and third blocks, printing over that made from the first lino cut. Ensure that the blocks are placed carefully within the pencil drawn frame (base sheet) and that the printing paper is always in alignment with the base sheet. By a process of progressive overprint, the multi-colour print is completed.

It is important to experiment with printing inks, their tonal qualities and transparency, in order to arrive at the most satisfactory colours and the order in which they should be printed.

Planographic printing

MONOPRINTS

There are two main methods of working:

1   Additive – ink or paint is applied directly to the surface of a tile. The tile should be perfectly flat, even surfaced and non-absorbent, for example, formica, glass or zinc plate. Images are developed by additions of colour.

2   Subtractive – the tile is covered with an even consistency of ink or paint using a roller. The required areas are then wiped away using fingers or cloths, or scratched out with the wooden end of a paint brush, a pencil or a thin stick such as a cocktail stick.

These two methods are often used in combination. Make a print in the usual manner. Place a clean sheet of newsprint or cartridge paper over the design. Hand pressure should be sufficient to make a clear impression.

A glass tile, although fragile, is particularly useful since a design/drawing can be prepared and placed under it. It is then possible to see the design as a guide to the application of colour.

REVERSE MONOPRINTS

Place a sheet of paper over printing ink rolled out on a tile. Draw on the paper with a pointed object (try using a ballpoint pen). Areas of soft shading can be created by rubbing gently over the paper with the fingers. When the paper is removed from the tile, the drawing will be seen in reverse on the underside.

Without adding any more ink, place another sheet of newsprint over the tile and rub over the back with your hand. Pull the paper away for a negative impression of the first print.

MASKING

Cut or torn paper or card shapes can be used to mask areas of printing ink that has been rolled out to an even consistency on a tile. When a sheet of paper is pressed over the ink, the paper or card shapes will act as masks and appear as the colour of the printing paper when the paper is removed.

Various materials could be used as masks including miscellaneous objects, feathers, lace, doilies, fabrics and leaves, separately or combined in designs.

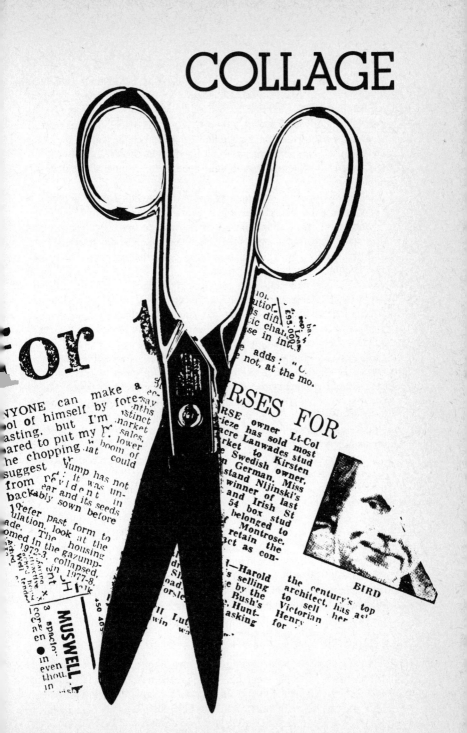

COLLAGE

George Braque is generally regarded as the first to have used *papier colle*. Together with Picasso, he developed the process to include various kinds of paper and cards including newspapers, wallpapers and sheet music. Dadaists and Surrealists were particularly important in stimulating interest in this new medium. It is a technique which all can attempt with ease. In the hands of artists such as Schwitters, who used thrown away objects such as bus tickets, labels and envelopes, it has many refinements and can become a completely satisfying technique.

Strong papers can be used as grounds for lightweight materials, otherwise cardboard, strawboard, hardboard, chipboard, plywood, linoleum, stretched fabric/canvas/hessian can be used. Pva binders are useful general purpose adhesives; *Copydex* and *Caretex* can be used for most fabrics. Further information on adhesives can be found in the Technical Notes section, page 74.

Before fixing materials into position, it is important to try different arrangements. Some organization is necessary although an accidental or spontaneous element can be exciting and valid. Each additional piece of paper or card that is stuck onto the main ground will change the relationship of the whole picture.

Whether the finished collage should be given a protective coating is a matter of preference. While a varnish (matt or gloss) will strengthen and make papers and cards waterproof, many artists leave their collages untreated to allow the colour and texture to remain authentic. Changes due to weathering and age, whilst leading to some deterioration in the materials used in the collage, have often renewed interest and created unexpected yet satisfactory qualities. Some artists have combined painting with collage not only for decorative purpose but also to provide a visual stimulant by the contrast or harmony of a real material substance with a painted surface. This was extended by Max Ernst to include frottage.

This form of art is sometimes known as 'the art of assemblage'. Since the early work of the Cubists in the 1910s, many different materials have been used including scraps of metal, wood and plastics and almost anything that came to hand. Picasso, in his Synthetic Cubist work, often used pieces of paper and other materials that involved some degree of projection from the canvas or board support, and a logical extension of this was the constructed relief.

Folded paper

Any kind of paper could be used but interesting tonal variations can be achieved when folding transparent or translucent papers. A sheet or shape of tissue paper (white), folded inward, over itself, from a number of points on its perimeter, will provide different degrees of tone especially when working with white paper to be fixed to a black base of sugar paper. The depth of tone will be related to the number of folds made. Use a clear paper adhesive sparingly, especially with thin papers.

Try combining this process with other collage processes. Torn and cut papers of various colours, textures and widths could be incorporated in the design. A linear effect or outline can be suggested by using thin strips of paper. Changes in direction can be made by folding the strip.

Creased paper - froissage

A technique which harnesses the possibilities of crinkled and creased paper shapes. Paper surfaces can be crinkled and then used in a design or pictorial composition, glued to the picture surface. It will provide contrasts with areas of flat sheets of paper. Try wetting the paper so that it becomes more malleable. Michael Fussell has used paper tissues soaked in emulsion paint (see his painting 'Kleenex', in the Tate Gallery) to create interesting tonal and textural statements. These have usually taken up twisting, swirling movements. The twists and wrinkles of the tissues became an important part of the overall effect. Alberto Burri has used hessian and Antonio Tapies a combination of materials including fabrics.

Emulsion and gloss paint will have their own powers of adhesion to hold tissue papers, paper towels and lightweight fabrics to a picture surface – preferably a board or card. Liquid tempera colour mixed with a little pva binder will serve well. Heavy papers will need to have glue applied to the underside to ensure a firm hold to the picture surface. Thinner papers such as tissue can be brushed over with a liquid adhesive (dilute pva binder). Alternatively the base board or card can be prepared with glue and the paper placed over it – further creasing would be possible while the glue is still wet.

Cut paper - découpage

There are two main features to note with this process: the use of clear, clean-cut outlines; and the variety of shapes cut from materials offering a range of textures and colours such as wallpaper, magazines, newspapers, rubbings, embossed and textured papers, glass or sand paper and crepe paper.

Careful thought should be given to the arrangement of the shapes. Try them in various positions on the base paper or card before making final decisions and fixing into position. Try making a collage with a 'family of shapes' – similar shapes but of different sizes. Shapes can be overlapped and, if transparent papers are used, variations in colour and tone achieved.

Representational imagery can be tried, using colours and textures which relate to an object or an idea. Stimulating and worthwhile work can also be created using colours for their own properties and for the relationships between them.

Cutting and folding back

Use scissors or a sharp knife to cut out parts of a sheet of paper or card so that they can be folded back from the position they occupied. Fix the cut-out shapes and the parent sheet to a card base. Positive and negative shapes are created and the original shape is extended. Try using paper or card with a different colour on each side; or white paper and a black paper or card base. An interesting interplay of shape and texture results from using paper textured on one side — try corrugated cardboard and textured wallpapers.

Shape extension

Cut a sheet of paper into a number of smaller shapes. Arrange the pieces into a design on a base paper or card by spacing them out while preserving their one to one relationships (ie, if pushed together again they would recreate the original overall shape). There are many variations that can be explored. Try incorporating the process in poster designs and illustrations. Early attempts could begin with basic geometric shapes — a square or a circle. With experience more adventurous explorations may produce bold and impressive designs, especially when textured and patterned papers are used.

Paper imitation mosaic

Small pieces of paper are used to create a design. It may be advisable to make a preliminary drawing or plan. Try working from the central area outwards. A quick way to collect small pieces is to cut the paper into strips (use off-cuts from previous use of the guillotine); then cut the strips into the appropriate lengths for the 'mosaic'. Brush paper glue onto an area of the base paper or card and then press the small pieces of paper into position. Irregular shapes may require a degree of overlapping of the mosaic pieces.

All kinds of papers can be used. The bright colours of glossy magazines, brochures and catalogues, and the tonal qualities of newspapers and photographs are possibilities.

Photocollage

To collect photo cuttings from magazines and newspapers, to arrange them on a base paper and fix them into position seems a fairly easy thing to do. In fact, it is one of the most difficult of the collage processes to do well. There are several ways of working including the following:

1   Cut a picture into sections then rearrange them in a different order to each other before fixing to a paper or card base. Variations in their proximity will add interesting spatial possibilities and degrees of tension between the shapes.

2   Use cuttings from a number of different pictures bringing them together in a new composition. Slots can be cut in some pictures or individual shapes into which other cut-out images can be inserted. Try to create an integrated compostion in which the parts seem to belong together. Optical illusion, fantasy, satire and wit can play a useful part in a photocollage as in the work of John Heartfield, the Dadaists and Surrealists such as Man Ray. A particular theme could be taken as a starting point; or photo-cuttings that are unconnected could be brought together in absurd, surreal relationships.

Veiling and overlapping

Pasting or glueing layers of paper on top of each other can be used to create variations in texture, tone, colour and shape. Transparent/translucent papers such as crepe, tissue, cellophane and sweet wrappers are useful for this technique. They can be used over other kinds of papers that have been previously glued to the base paper or card. Cut, torn, wrinkled and folded papers can be incorporated. One or two basic shapes and colours will produce a variety of new shapes, textures and colours. It is advisable to start with a limited range otherwise the work may become too complex and get out of hand. A clear paper glue should be used sparingly, or it may leave unwanted marks and wrinkles in the paper.

Try using this process over photocollage. Interesting effects can result by veiling parts of faces and objects. It is also a useful way of exploring colour and tonal relationships.

Torn paper-déchirage

Torn paper shapes can be used as alternatives in all the collage processes. The frayed or rough edges offer a quality very different to the clean cut edges of shapes cut with a knife or scissors. They are particularly useful in overlapping, layering or veiling processes. The tearing of the paper or card is difficult to control and a random element is involved. A greater degree of control can be gained by tearing in the direction of the vein or water mark which is present in most papers. The pieces can be employed in imaginative picture making, on their own or combined with painting; or arranged to create interesting designs. Most papers and cards can be used. Arrange the torn shapes on the base paper or card before fixing with a paper glue such as *Gloy* or a pva binder thinned with a little water.

Examples of the déchirage technique are to be seen in the environment, though often of a somewhat accidental nature, for example, on billboards. Déchirage has been used by a number of artists including Robert Motherwell.

Miscellaneous materials

Very many 'ready made' materials, mainly two-dimensional in character, offer exciting possibiilites for use in collage work. Of natural objects, leaves, petals, grasses, reeds, 'flat' shells, feathers and bark offer potential. Man-made objects that could be considered include tickets, labels (see 'Opened by Customs' by Kurt Schwitters — plate 9), envelopes, wrapping papers, stamps, foil paper, negatives and photographs, drinking straws, pieces of machinery, insides of clocks and watches, and milk bottle tops.

The materials could relate to a particular subject matter or they might suggest ideas for compositions. As well as being used in their natural state, they could be cut, torn, creased or folded. A pva binder is a suitable adhesive as are *Uhu* and *Bostick*. Hardboard, plywood or strawboard could be used as a base.

Other possibilities

1 Take rubbings from the collage designs using a sheet of newsprint and a thick wax crayon (see Rubbings page 44).

2 Printmaking — apply printing ink to the surface of a collage design using a roller. Place a clean sheet of paper over the design and press using a clean roller or a rag and hand pressure (see Printmaking — Paper print, page 48, Cut card print and Waste block printing page 49).

3 Collect rubbings made from textures in the environment. Cut or tear them into shapes to be arranged on a base paper or card (see Rubbings page 44).

4 Combine several collage techniques in one work.

5 Use rug, carpet and/or lino oddments. The thicker they are the more they will approximate to low relief work. Strong scissors or a sharp craft knife will be needed, These materials are not suitable for young children to use unless the oddments are first cut by an adult. A board base is advised.

MOSAICS

Traditionally, mosaic is a process of using small pieces of material inlaid in a 'bed', perhaps of cement or plaster, so that they become part of the surface. The term has come to be used to describe the process of fixing small pieces of a material on the top of a surface. Mosaic art reached a high standard in the work of Byzantines in the eleventh and twelfth centuries. Perhaps the most exciting work was done by the Aztecs whose favourite material was turquoise (see plate 15 for an example of modern Mexican mosaic work). Buildings have been decorated with mosiacs and the Aztecs used them for religious objects, medallions, mirrors, masks, shields and knife handles. Mosaic pieces have been stuck onto a variety of surfaces such as pottery, wood, shells and leather. Possibilities for practical work could include the following.

Mosaic beds

SAND AND PASTE BASE   Mix the sand with Polycell (instead of the traditional cement or lime). A firm base is needed such as plywood, chipboard or hardboard, (cardboard tends to buckle), with battens fixed around the perimeter. Pour the sand/paste mixture into the wooden base to cover it completely to a depth of approximately 3 cm. The paste retards drying and allows time for placing the mosaic pieces into position — try using pebbles, beads or bottle tops. It is advisable to begin with the outlines of shapes, using the pieces that are most in contrast to the sand/paste mix. Set the pieces close together. Large forms will usually look well against the plain sand base. Do not move the completed mosaic until it has dried.

CEMENT   Make a mixture of one part sand to one part cement and add water to a thick consistency. Pour the mixture into a frame on a hardboard base (see above). Stones, pieces of coloured glass and broken pottery could be used to create a design pressed into the cement. Leave the panel to harden.

PLASTIC CEMENT   Use a trowel to make a bed, 3 cm in depth, of a plastic cement such as Nic-o-Bond in a wooden frame which has been fixed — glued or nailed — to a board base. Press the chosen mosaic pieces into position. Nic-o-Bond dries in three to four hours but it is advisable to leave it for a few days before moving the mosaic to ensure that it is completely dry.

BOARD BASE   Use an all purpose adhesive such as Uhu or Evostick Clear to glue the mosaic pieces to a board base. If the panel is to be suspended on a wall the 'hangers' should be fixed into position before applying the mosaic design to the board surface. It is advisable to seal the board against damp with varnish, resin or a pva binder. Variations of this technique could include mosaics on bottles, trays, boxes, lids and belts.

PLASTER   It is possible to use plaster of Paris in the same way as the sand/paste base. There may be difficulties when the plaster starts to set and it will be necessary to work fast. The rate of setting can be retarded by adding four or five teaspoons of vinegar to the plaster mix or by using more water than usual.

An alternative method is to make a wooden frame (side wall depth at least 7.5 cm) for the perimeter of the design. Press the frame into a bed of clay that is slightly larger in area than the frame – a hardboard base could be used for the clay. The mosaic pieces should then be pressed into the clay, remembering that the design will be in reverse. Mix the plaster in a bowl (see Technical Notes page 85): pour the plaster into the frame to a depth of about 5 cm.

Ensure that the plaster has set before removing the frame and the clay. Wash the front of the panel to remove clay stains and grout between the pieces. A coat of varnish could be applied if desired.

NEWCLAY   is a clay mixed with nylon fibres which does not have to be fired in a kiln. It can be used on a large or a small scale – for example for making paper weights. Use the lids of cartons (for example, cheese boxes) and press the Newclay into the lid mould to make a base. Pasta, seeds, beads or buttons, arranged into a design, can be pressed into position in the Newclay. The nearer the pieces are together the firmer the surface will be. Brush the finished surface with a pva binder to obviate the tendency for the pieces to fall out as the moisture in the Newclay evaporates.

Mosaic materials

Scrap or waste materials can be used such as plastic, metal wood, clock pieces, bicycle and car parts. On a smaller scale, washers, beads, beans, seeds, pasta and shells make interesting surfaces.

SHELLS   Use the tougher shells – winkles, whelks, mussels, cockles, scallops, and saddle oysters. They can be glued to a wooden base, a stone (paper-weight), or embedded in Newclay. The strongest shells could be tried in sand/paste or plastic cement.

PEBBLES   The most obvious source is the beach, but all manner of pebbles can be used. Due regard should be given to the overall weight. The pebbles can be embedded in all the substances suggested or glued to a board base.

BOTTLE GLASS   Care will be needed when handling sharp edges. A safe way of breaking empty bottles is by either laying them inside thick brown paper or between layers of hessian/sacking. Mild hammer blows should be sufficient to make small pieces without smashing them into smithereens. Bottle glass could be tried with any of the mosaic beds mentioned above.

TRANSPARENT GLASS   Pieces of coloured glass are glued to transparent glass (perspex off-cuts could be used) using a clear adhesive, for example, *Bostick, Uhu* or epoxy resin. The coloured pieces could be arranged according to a design previously worked on paper placed underneath the pane of glass. Putty could be used in the dividing lines if desired. The completed design is likely to look well as a transparency against a light source or placed in a picture frame. If it is to be used as a window outside, a clear epoxy resin must be used as an adhesive.

Scrap glass can be obtained from stained glass studios or, occasionally, from a glass merchant.

Stained glass can be bought as off-cuts and is usually cheaper in this form than when bought in complete sheets. It can be used in any of the methods described. It is at its best when used as a window or transparency. *Polyfilla*, mixed with black liquid tempera colour or lamp black powder, could be used between the glass pieces if desired.

TESSERAE   Thin, square pieces of opaque glass or stained glass can be cut from sheets (or from off-cuts) using a glass cutter. It is easier to purchase commercial tesserae which can be bought loose by the pound, or fixed to a paper backing. It is possible to make tesserae yourself from clay if you have access to a kiln. Plaster of Paris can also be used. Mix powder colour with a little water and add this to the water to be used when mixing the plaster of Paris to a smooth paste. This has to be done without delay since the plaster will set in a short time. Pour the coloured plaster into a wooden frame on a board base (lino or glass could be used as a base first brushed with a thin coating of soap as an insulating layer; use wooden battens or clay as walls around the edges of the base). While the plaster is setting, make horizontal or vertical cuts to make mosaic squares to the desired size. When the plaster has hardened, the squares can be detached from the base with a palette knife or a spatula. The home made tesserae could be tried in any of the mosaic methods described.

SMALTI   Opaque glass cubes, substitutes for which include home made clay or plaster cubes, can be used successfully in any of the mosaic processes described. If they are used in a regular pattern, choice of colour relationships will be important especially if the smalti are all of the same size. A variety of sizes could be tried. Contrasts of tone, colour, shape and texture can be harnessed to help create an exciting and interesting design. If a figurative subject is chosen the pieces could be arranged to follow the main lines of direction or action of the figure(s).

RELIEF
TECHNIQUES

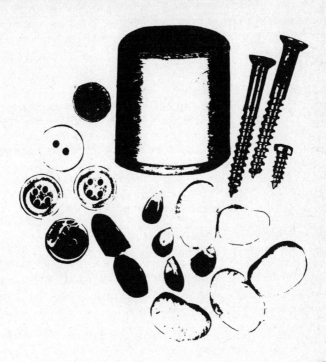

There are only fine distinctions between collage and relief, and between relief and sculpture. Whereas with collage the two-dimensional nature of the base, ground or picture surface is preserved, in making a relief panel the materials fixed to the base may project away from it to a range of distances. A strong base is needed such as hardboard, plywood or blockboard; card or strong paper could be used as a base for light-weight materials such as papers and feathers.

Paper

FOLDED PAPER RELIEF
Use a sharp cutting knife to cut openings in a sheet of cartridge or sugar paper (rest the paper on a cutting board for this operation); leave the paper hinged to the parent sheet. Fold back the hinged shapes. Some of them could be hinged to project outward when a directional light source will be important.

Try a figurative design, based perhaps on natural subject matter such as a bird, fish, or a butterfly. Cut into the paper and fold or roll it back to create details of feathers, scales or markings.

MULTI-PIECE PAPER RELIEF
The relief is made by adding forms that have been cut or folded in paper and fixed to a base card or board – use a paper glue or a pva binder, or fix into position by plaiting or slotting.

Boxes

Arrange small boxes – cheese, match, and cigar boxes are useful – into a design on a base board. Fix them into position with a pva binder. When the adhesive is dry they can be painted using a brush and liquid tempera colour mixed with a little pva binder, or spray painted. If preferred, the boxes could be painted individually before fixing into position.

Use the lids of larger boxes – for example, shoe and hat boxes, as the bases for designs created with other materials, arranged and fixed into position.

Tubes

Cardboard centres, such as those of toilet rolls, carpets and maps, can be used to create a design in relief, fixed into place on a base board using a pva binder. Strawboard or hardboard are suitable as a baseboard. The tubes can be painted before fixing to the base or the relief design can be painted when the adhesive is dry. The more the tubes (or sections cut from them), placed horizontally or vertically, project away from the base the nearer they are to being sculpture.

Buttons

Use either buttons only or buttons in combination with other materials. Make a design to be stuck onto a two-dimensional surface such as hardboard, blockboard or strawboard; or to decorate constructions. Fix the buttons into position using a pva binder. It is worthwhile exploring the different sizes, textures and colours of the buttons, especially where contrasts are required in the designs. (see Mosaics – Newclay, page 61).

Bark

Choose pieces of bark that will lie reasonably flat. The colours, shapes and textures should be considered in the design before fixing the bark pieces to a base board. Twigs, cut to the desired length, could be used in combination with the bark. (see Collage – Miscellaneous materials, page 58).

Seeds

The wide variety of seed types provides a good choice of colour and size. Fruit pips such as melon, orange, lemon, apple and grapefruit should be dried before use. They can be used alone or in combination with other materials such as pasta, lentils, bark, buttons, dried grasses and leaves. Brush an adhesive – pva binder is suitable – over a card or board base (a small area at a time) and apply the seeds to it. The design could evolve as the work progresses, or be drawn first on the base before the adhesive is applied. (see Mosaics – Newclay page 61; and Collage – Miscellaneous materials, page 58).

Miscellaneous and waste materials

These include cotton reels, cardboard packets, parts of clocks and watches, matchsticks, bottle-caps, metal scrap, linoleum and egg boxes. It is possible to use all the different materials in combination but it is advisable to use similar materials together in one piece of work. This makes for ease of working and less confusion when maintaining control of the progress of a design. It also leads to ease of choice of an adhesive (although a pva binder or *Uhu* is a good all purpose adhesive).

Any one of the found or waste materials could be used alone in the creation of a relief panel. For example, egg boxes used whole, in half boxes and individual segments, can be arranged into a design on a base board. They could be placed close to each other to cover the whole of the base; or, if spaces are left between them, these could be painted or collage added. Layers of parts of the boxes can be built one on top of another. Once the adhesive has dried, the relief can be painted using a brush or a spray gun.

Egg shells, although fragile, can be used to create worthwhile relief panels. Use half shells: they can be used either way up or on their sides to give contrast in area and height of projection. Smaller pieces will help to give a richer overall texture. The surfaces of the shells can be coloured using water-based paint or inks — use a soft-haired brush, for example, squirrel or sable hair. The shells can also be coloured with a felt tip pen. It is important that any adhesive used for fixing the shells is dry before colouring is applied. Too much pressure with pen or brush may damage the shells.

There are very many materials that could be used as alternatives or in addition to those already mentioned, such as: tin cans, iron filings, chicken wire, metal foil, wire, nails, nuts and bolts, glass, sand, perspex, polystyrene, cork, woodshavings, woodblocks, nuts and nutshells, drinking straws, plaster and clay. Wherever possible costs can be reduced by using off-cuts of, for example, perspex, wood and metal sheeting.

Nail relief

Use wood as a base — thick blockboard makes a good base as there is less risk of the wood splitting. A preliminary drawing could be made on the wood. If the surface of the wood is to be cleaned and polished, this should be done before applying the nails. The nails are more likely to reflect the light if they are inserted at different angles and heights. Tacks and drawing pins will help to give greater variety of colour, texture, height and size of 'head'.

Fine examples of nail relief can be seen in the work of David Partridge.

Wood block relief

Wood blocks, arranged into a design on a wood or board base, can be fixed into position with a pva binder. Joe Tilson has produced much exciting, sensitive work using these materials, in which he has explored the subtle colour and textural qualities of the wood and the importance of light and shade affected by the careful placement of the blocks (plate 14). Use sandpaper to remove rough edges; and it is as well to polish the wood blocks before fixing them into position on the base.

Wire

Soft iron wire is suitable for this process, but any kind of wire could be tried. Use hardboard, blockboard or plywood as a base. Hammer nails into and around the edge of the board (it is usual to place them equidistant, but the intervals could be varied for particular ideas or to explore possibilities). Wire can be stretched across the board between the nails, and fixed into position by winding the ends round the nails and twisting, using a pair of pliers. Further lengths of wire can be woven in and out of the wire grid to add to the design and to create areas of interest or focal points. For more permanence, the wire lengths could be joined using a soldering iron.

Clay

There are three main processes to try in context here:

1 Making impressions in the clay (at least 2.5 cm thick) by using fingers or other simple implements.

2 Adding clay to the surface of a clay block or tile. Ensure careful jointing of the clay – use of a 'slip' will help.

3 Parts of a clay tile or block can be scooped out to create a design or figurative composition.

The work can be fired in a kiln to earthenware temperature; or, if it is *Newclay*, allowed to harden and sealed with a varnish or with a pva binder; or a plaster cast can be made of it (see below).

Plaster relief cast made from a mould

The mould could be of a variety of materials such as clay, plasticene or lino-cuts.

A negative cast is made when the plaster is poured directly onto and over the relief panel or object. A positive cast requires that the relief panel be pressed into a mould such as clay or plasticene. For example, press a lino cut into a clay tile (approximately 2.5 cm thick) to leave an impression in the clay, which has now formed the mould ready to receive the plaster. Build a wall round the mould using cardboard, wood or clay (about 2.5 cm higher than the surface of the mould). The wall must be strong enough to contain the plaster; and there must not be any gaps (plug with clay or plasticene) through which the plaster can escape. A cardboard box will serve well. Fill the box with a 2.5 – 7 cm layer of clay, and smooth and flatten the surface. Press objects (or the relief panel or lino-cut) into the clay. They will have to be carefully removed to avoid distorting the impressions. Mix the plaster (see the

Technical Notes, page 85) and pour it over the clay to a thickness of 2.5 − 5 cm, leave it to set for approximately 40 minutes. Do not leave it so long that the clay hardens, since it will then be more difficult to remove from the plaster. Remove the cardboard box or the wall; carefully separate the plaster from the clay and wash the plaster block to clean it of traces of clay.

If the final plaster relief is to be hung on a wall, it will need a loop to suspend it from. A length of wire or string bent into a loop can be placed just below the surface of the plaster while it is still soft, just before it sets, leaving part of the loop exposed.

Embedding – materials set into a plaster panel or block

The chosen materials or objects are pressed into a block of plaster immediately before the plaster hardens. It is important to have decided on the arrangement of the objects before making the plaster block. Once the plaster starts to set there will be little time for alterations to be made. The objects can be placed into the plaster so that they are partially projecting into space whilst held in position when the plaster finally hardens.

A cast plaster block can be made by pouring the liquid plaster into a box as in casting from a mould. The objects are arranged and left slightly impressed in the clay bed to become part of the block surface as the plaster sets.

Wax or clay cast from plaster

The smooth surface of a block of plaster can be scored or engraved with a sharp tool. The design can be outlined in pencil first. It is then carved or scraped out of the plaster block. When the design is complete, ensure that the chippings are removed and that the surface of the plaster is smooth and clean. Press glitter wax into the plaster mould, or place a frame round the plaster block (for example, a lid of a cardboard box) before applying hot melted wax to make a cast.

Clay is easier to use in small scale work, pressed into the plaster mould; but the surface of the plaster must be kept damp and the cast removed before the clay dries.

Plaster casts from plaster moulds

(See Plaster relief cast from a mould page 67). The mould has to be prepared by applying a coating of soap with a brush or wet rag. Avoid the formation of air bubbles by wiping off traces of foam. With a well fitting frame around the mould, pour in the plaster mix for the cast.

When the plaster has set, the cast can be detached. Gentle taps along the join when the plaster is absolutely dry should soon separate obstinate adhesions.

A plaster cylinder from a mould

Pour the plaster mixture (see Technical Notes, page 85) into a cardboard tube, perhaps the centre of a toilet or kitchen towel roll, or a jam jar. When the plaster has hardened, cut, tear or pull the cardboard away or crack the jam jar (care will be needed – try wrapping the jar in newspaper to avoid injury from splinters). Carve or engrave a design in the plaster cylinder.

A relief panel can be obtained by rolling the engraved plaster cylinder over a clay tile which is slightly wider than the cylinder and approximately 2 cm thick. The clay can be fired in a kiln to earthenware temperature having first removed all traces of plaster; or left to harden if *Newclay* is used. The *Newclay* can be coloured by painting with liquid tempera colour mixed with a little pva binder.

Foil relief

Place a sheet of foil (for example, baking foil) over a firm and resilient support such as thick felt or several layers of newspapers or wallpaper off-cuts. Use a pencil, ballpoint pen or other implement to make impressions into the foil, being careful not to break the surface. This will be the reverse of the design. When the work is completed, turn the foil over and fix it to a card or strawboard base using a pva binder.

Punched metal design-repoussage

Use tin plate over a thick piece of board so that the punches or nails do not penetrate the tin and damage the table or work bench surface. The design can be drawn out first by scratching with a fine point. Use a hammer and metal punches or nails to make impressions in the surface of the tin plate. Any sharp areas that occur around the impressions made can be carefully filed down.

Where possible use a dense rubber support instead of a block of wood. Also, try to avoid using nails which tend to pierce the surface of the metal. A round-ended tool for raising curved areas and a finer tool for chasing and areas of detailed linear decoration are preferable.

Different metals could be used, such as aluminium or copper but these are very expensive. The sheets of metal should be less than 0.2 mm thick.

SOME OTHER PROCESSES TO TRY

Photograms

The basic method is to expose areas of a sheet of light sensitive photographic paper to a strong light source. Use opaque or semi-opaque objects to mask parts of the paper. The areas masked will appear white, the remainder will have turned to various degrees of grey. The masking must be done in a darkened room. A safe light will be necessary – a red light bulb or a torchlight covered with red cellophane – to see by when arranging the objects on the sensitive side of the paper. The paper is then exposed to a light source – the controlled light source of an enlarger, a desk light or torch light – approximately 1.5 – 2 m from the paper. Expose to the light for about 30 seconds. Experiment to find the desired length of exposure time which may vary according to the paper used, the strength of the light, the distance of the paper from the light source and the translucency of the objects to be placed on the photographic paper. Switch off the light and develop and fix in safe-light conditions. Wash the print in water, preferably running water, then dry, between blotting paper, for example, if a commercial dryer is not available, or pegged on an indoor line.

Three plastic trays will be needed, one each for the developer, fixer and water. Follow the manufacturer's instructions when using developer and fixer. Use plastic tongs to remove the photogram from one tray to another.

Variations of the process include:

1   Squeeze ink between two sheets of glass; place on top of the photographic paper and proceed as above. The masks achieved are of an accidental nature. Objects could be placed on top of the glass before exposing to the light source.

2   Hand-drawn negatives. Make a drawing on transparent paper (tracing paper, thin drawing paper or thin clear plastic). Place the drawing, now the negative, onto the photographic paper in safe-light conditions. Expose to a light source. Then develop, fix, wash and dry. Every mark drawn onto the 'negative' will appear in reverse – a black drawn line will be white after printing.

3   Collage and miscellaneous objects – stick paper shapes or objects such as leaves or feathers onto the transparent sheet and proceed as in (2) above.

Projector slides

The basic method is to project onto a screen experiments with coloured transparent and translucent materials such as cellophane, tissue paper, thin fabrics, plastics, slivers of fruits and peel, petals and leaves. Cut two pieces of cardboard each 5 cm square for use with a slide projector, or 25 cm x 20 cm if using an overhead projector. Cut corresponding

71

windows in the pair of chosen size. Alternatively, for a slide projector, slide frames can be purchased. Sandwich the chosen materials between two pieces of sellotape or *Transpaseal* cut to size. Put the *Transpaseal/* sellotape between the cards; and seal the edges with sellotape. Project onto a screen. For an overhead projector an alternative method for making a slide would be as follows. Place a sheet of manilla card (25 x 20 cm), from which a window has been cut (leaving a 3 cm frame), onto a sheet of self-adhesive transparent plastic, such as *Transpaseal*, of the same size. The coloured materials should then be placed within the frame, to adhere to the *Transpaseal*. Place a second sheet of *Transpaseal* over the surface to seal the design. The 'slide' can now be used on the overhead projector. As well as projecting the design onto a screen, try projecting it at different angles onto different surfaces — walls, ceilings, boxes and other objects and onto people.

A moving slide can be made by using two liquids that will not mix. Make a plastic envelope of two pieces of clear perspex, each 5 cm square, placed together and sealed round three edges with sellotape or *Transpaseal*. The joints must be strong to prevent any seepage. Inject two liquids, such as washing-up liquid or coloured ink and bicycle oil or brake fluid. Seal the opening. Project the slide onto a screen or other chosen surface. Experiment with liquids to decide preferences.

Old photographic negatives can be used as projector slides. Scratch a design in the emulsion on the matt side of the negative using a pointed instrument — a pen knife, a needle (insert the 'eye' end into a cork for ease of handling) or lino-cutting tools. The original images on the negatives can be further obscured by using two together, placed with the emulsion side inwards. They can be sealed together with sellotape.

Try scratching a design on unwanted slide transparencies which have the advantage of being already framed for use in the projector.

Marbling

Use a brush to lay waterproof inks, or oil colours thinned with turpentine, onto the surface of water that is in a trough or a tray (an old baking tin will suffice). The longer the brush is left on the water the more the colour will tend to spread. A separate brush should be used for each colour. The colours will be moving on the surface of the water which could be stirred gently with the wooden end of a paint brush. Carefully lower one edge of a sheet of paper that will just fit into the trough onto the surface of the water and gradually lower the whole sheet to rest on the water. Lift the paper straightaway, with a rolling action from one end. This technique is traditionally used for the end-papers of books, bookcovers, wallpapers and mounts for greetings cards. Collage could be added to the marbling, for example, cuttings from magazines or wallpapers.

An alternative is to spray enamel paint onto the surface of the water and then proceed as above.

Greater control over the marbling process can be exerted by using a 'size' instead of water. *Carragheen* moss size will provide a thicker surface onto which colour can be dropped and spread using a comb. The patterns will be transferred onto the paper laid onto the surface.

Coloured cement inlay

Cement and sand – one part cement to two parts of sand – are mixed with water to a thick consistency. Dye some of the mixture with liquid powder colours. Arrange the coloured cement into a design on a suitable base – plywood, hardboard, a pane of glass or lino. Distinct areas are advised rather than intricate designs. The plain cement is then applied over the design to an appreciable thickness to form a block. Allow two or three days for drying, then the whole block can be lifted from the base. Cement, although it takes a long time to set, does not adhere to the base.

Stucco inlay

Make a plaster block (see Technical Notes – Plaster mixing page 85). A design can be drawn on the plaster with a pencil and then retraced with a sharp instrument. The areas to be inlaid should then be scraped away with a knife to a depth of approximately 1.5 cm and filled with a liquid mixture of coloured plaster (add a little powder colour when mixing the plaster). Each area should be separately treated, filled in and left to dry. Care will be needed to ensure that the coloured plaster does not spill onto the white plaster surface.

Technical notes

Adhesives

Cold water pastes, under various trade names, are satisfactory for general purposes and can be kept for some time if mixed with a few crystals of permanganate of potash. *Gloy*, *Uhu* and *Copydex* can be used for most papers; and *Copydex* and *Caretex* for most textiles. *Cow Gum* is useful where it is necessary to pull apart surfaces previously joined. *Evostick Impact Adhesive* is good for non-porous surfaces such as metal and stone. *Evostick Clear* will stick most things but it reacts against foam polystyrene. *Unibond*, however, can be used with polystyrene. *Gluak* holds immediately and is useful when making lightweight constructions as are *Uhu* and *Caretex*. *Polycell* is a good seal for porous surfaces, particularly for thinner papers; it keeps well.

Uhu and pva binders are good all-purpose adhesives. *Uhu* will glue anything with the exception of polythene and polystyrene. Pva binders, such as *Marvin Medium* and *Evostick Wood Working* adhesive, can be used with polystyrene and are particularly useful for collage work. They should be diluted for use with thinner papers; and they do not cause tissue papers to bleed as do many other adhesives (they should not be diluted by more than a third with water).

There are many different adhesives available and it is important to read manufacturers' instructions carefully before use. It is also important to clean brushes (and other applicators) thoroughly, especially when using pva binders which, when dry, will render the brushes virtually useless.

Brushes

Different jobs need different brushes. Brushes are sold in a range of sizes indicated by numbers (usually 0-12, from small to large) or by width (1in – 4in. for most purposes). There are also different shapes: pointed, round, flat and filbert (tapered).

BRUSHES USED IN PAINTING   These are usually made from the hair of different animals, such as hog, ox, squirrel and sable. Brushes made from synthetic materials such as nylon are also available.

Hog hair bristle brushes can be used with oil colours – long flat shape and filbert shape, and with powder and liquid tempera colours – with the addition of the round shaped brushes.

Ox hair brushes are best used with water-based paints such as poster colours and gouache. Of the softer haired brushes, sable are the better quality and the most expensive but with care will last a life time. They are well worth the investment. Squirrel, ox and bear hair brushes are useful for most work to be done with water-based media. Of these, squirrel hair brushes are the cheapest and serve especially well with water colours.

Decorators' brushes can be stiff or soft and are useful for large scale work. As with the larger hog hair brushes, they are good for bold, freer work.

BRUSHES USED FOR PASTING   Although any of the brushes already mentioned could be used, it would be sensible to use the cheapest. There are also special flat paste brushes often made of nylon.

GLUE BRUSHES   The hog hair bristle and the decorators brushes mentioned above can be used with glues. Special round glue brushes are wired for reinforcement and are especially recommended if hot water glues and sizes are being used on large areas. Clean the brushes thoroughly. They should never be left to stand on their bristles; and are best kept horizontally in a shallow tray.

Colour palette

The range of colour to be used will depend on individual preferences and the demands of the work in hand. With practice, preferred colours will be determined and added to a basic palette. Start with the following which are ample for successful painting.

TEMPERA COLOURS   and other water-based media:

Vermillion *

Crimson

Brilliant Yellow *

Ultramarine *

Viridian

Burnt Umber *

Yellow Ochre

Black *

White *

The list could be reduced further if necessary to those colours marked with an asterisk. The range can be gradually developed with subsequent work.

OIL COLOURS   sold in tins or tubes. Rowney's School of Art colour in half pint tins is good value for use in schools where it is expected that a fair amount of oil painting will be done.

There are different tube sizes. It would be sensible to buy larger sized tubes of those colours likely to be more used. The following would be a good palette to begin with, remembering that personal preferences are important. Recommended tube sizes are in brackets.

Flake or Titanium White (14)

Yellow Ochre (8)

Chrome Yellow (8)

Cadmium Red (8)

Cobalt Blue (8)

Ivory Black (8)

Most likely additions are: Ultramarine, Lemon Yellow, Viridian, Burnt Sienna, Vermillion and Raw Umber. It is important to use non-toxic colours in the classroom. Check manufacturer's instructions before purchasing.

For household emulsion and oil paints, a different range of names is given to the colours available. Selection should be made after consulting a manufacturer's colour chart.

The arrangement of colours on the mixing palette can be important to a good ordered system of working. Place warm colours to one side of white with yellows next, progressing to reds and browns; and, cold colours on the other side including greens, blues and black.

Painting knives

The best painting knives are those made from one piece of forged steel, straight or trowel shaped, usually set in a wooden handle. Avoid those that are welded as they have a tendency to break at the join which is usually made at the heel of the blade. Some manufacturers of artist's materials are putting on the market cheaper plastic knives which are quite suitable for beginners. A straight-blade knife might be said to be an extension of the painter's arm and a more direct way of applying paint. A trowel-shaped blade requires more control, and is capable of a wider range of marks and affords fine subtlety of colour.

It is possible to complete a painting with one knife but it is advisable to have a basic set of three. A large, long, straight blade is useful for making sweeping strokes for the largest areas of a painting and for under-painting (such a knife could also be used for cleaning the mixing palette). A smaller blade, 10 cm in length approximately, would be necessary for colour mixing. Details will require a slimmer blade to suggest, for example, the masts of ships, windows and roof tiles of small buildings, street furniture and figures in a landscape. The triangular or trowel-shaped blades are the most suitable for suggesting textural qualities of clothing, rock structures, scaffolding and walls. The painting knife should have a blade that tapers. It will be needed for different kinds of marks in the painting.

Underpainting and the first layers of paint should be applied with the least flexible of the straight blades. Pressure is needed to force undiluted paint into the pores of a canvas or other rough surface. When working on paper or card this is not so necessary, but the straight, stiffer blade is still the most suitable for the application of broader areas of colour. The larger the painting the larger the knife to be used for underpainting. The largest is most commonly 20 cm in length. A blade of 10 cm in length is useful for medium-sized paintings.

The degree of flexibility in the blade is important. It is not possible to spread the paint accurately with a blade that is too flexible and weak. On the other hand, a blade that is too stiff requires more pressure to apply the paint which will then ooze out from underneath the knife and not remain where intended.

Details can best be stated either using a pointed trowel-shaped blade of 5–7 cm long, or a stiff pointed blade (such as a penknife). The first is good for working into wet paint; and it is useful for working over thicker layers of underpainting. The second is helpful when dealing with smaller areas and marks, especially when using the edge of the blade for lines, and the tip or point for small marks such as facial details in portraiture.

A good general purpose knife is one of 12–15 cm long with a straight flexible blade. It is useful for mixing colours on the palette, blending colours whilst they are still wet on the picture surface and for smoothing out unwanted textures.

After some experience of painting with knives you will be able to decide which knives you prefer. The smaller trowel-shaped, flexible blades are often rejected by artists as paint applicators because they are thought to be too thin and difficult to control the paint with. Nevertheless they can be useful and the least flexible of them can be a good choice for stating certain areas of detail, for example, in flower studies, landscapes, hair and clothing in portraiture, as well as providing interesting textural qualities. They have been used successfully for mixing pigment with an oil vehicle and for mixing colour with additives such as french chalk.

It is important that knives should be kept clean. Paint that has been allowed to dry on a blade will injure the paint film when the knife is next used. This may result in an uneven layer of colour and cause unnecessary frustrations. Keep a rag near to hand to clean a blade immediately after use.

Painting media

Any pigment or painting media that is soluble in water is known as a water-based medium.

WATER COLOURS – TRANSPARENT

These are usually available in tablet form or in tubes. Colours of artist's quality tend to be expensive. The tablets of colour are often to be seen in water-colour boxes, the lids of which form useful mixing trays.

Transparent colours will be most effective when painting on a white ground which will reflect most light. The eye sees a result of the light passing through the colour to the white ground which reflects it back through the colour to the eye. The white of the ground, usually paper, will be the lightest area in a painting. Colour is lightened and thinned by adding more water. A direct approach is usually the most successful with details added towards the end of a process. Too much overpainting tends to result in a loss of colour brilliance. However, an effect similar to that of glazing with oil colours can be achieved by painting layers of transparent washes – each layer of paint should be dry before the next is applied.

WATER COLOURS – OPAQUE

The addition of chinese white or chalk will make transparent water colours opaque. A gum medium is added as a binder. To lighten opaque colour, white is added rather than water. Black (which is not usually used with transparent colours) will help to neutralise contrasting areas of opaque colour. It should be noted that black will not only darken colours but will also influence the colour property; for instance, yellows appear as greens and reds become browns. When mixing opaque colours, it is important to allow for the fact that they will dry much lighter than they appear when wet.

The cleaning of applicators after use with opaque colours should include washing with soap. This is to ensure all the gum content of the media has been removed.

Working with water colours on wet paper can be satisfying. Apart from the possibility of interesting imagery as the paint flows or spreads into different colour mixtures and shapes, the paper will mark more easily when wet. Although such a mark will be difficult to remove, the process can be worthwhile, requiring rapid action since the paper will dry quickly. A mark made on wet paper breaks the surface and causes the paper to become more absorbent. When colour is applied it will remain darker where the paper surface has been broken. There are two main methods:

1   Apply a colour wash then scratch the surface by drawing into it,

for instance with a pencil, cocktail stick, finger nail or palette knife; or

2   Draw onto the wet paper before applying colour.

TEMPERA COLOURS

These are in use in powder, liquid or paste form. They are easy and convenient to use and cheaper than oils though lacking the same colour intensity and flexibility. Powder colours are preferable to ready-mixed colours since they encourage colour mixing, particularly of secondary and tertiary colours, and facilitate the experience and understanding of colour properties and consistencies. Their granular nature can be useful for different textural qualities.

Liquid and paste tempera colours stay bright and clean after mixing. The tendency for tempera, especially powder colours, to dry flatter and duller than when wet and to have a slight chalky appearance can be alleviated by mixing them to a creamy consistency (to that of yoghurt is usually thick enough). They are fast drying; and the absorbency of paper surfaces increases the drying rate. This can be an advantage, making it possible to work on a painting for a longer time than when using oils in any one sitting. But a disadvantage is that there is less opportunity to alter or correct colour statements. Once colour has been absorbed into the surface of a paper it is difficult to remove — a damp cloth or sponge will take off some of the unwanted colour.

Ready-mixed liquid colour is suitable and reliable for most of the painting techniques suggested in this book. It is useful for painting with fingers, sponges and rags and can be used with spray guns and in action painting.

POSTER COLOURS

The picture ground can be completely hidden by poster paint, and its opacity can be increased by the addition of white if required when overpainting. It is usually sold in pots or tubes but is also available in solid cakes or blocks. The latter have certain disadvantages: they are not suited to thick impasto and the paint film is often thin. Valuable time and spontaneity can be lost whilst 'working-up' enough colour from the block. They tend to increase the effects of wear on sponges and brushes. The pots of paint are the easiest to use and keep in good condition; you may need a knife to take the required amount from the pot.

The paint can be spread in different thicknesses. Transparency can be achieved by thinning colours with water. In this way they are useful for planning a composition. Ideas can be stated on the picture ground fluently and quickly. Later stages should be thicker. As soon as the colour is dry, further applications can be painted over it. To preserve the colour intensity of the last layer it should be thicker

79

than the previous application. Poster paint will not crumble or crack as easily as liquid tempera when applied impasto. It should be noted that overworking with an applicator can disturb paint already applied. It is best to think first and use a direct application of paint, placing it where desired and leaving it be.

Poster colours dry lighter and may appear chalky where white has been mixed with darker hues; you should make allowances for this when mixing. Poster colours can be used with comparative ease, without too much concern with technical problems. They are inexpensive compared with oils. There is a wide range of colours available so that there is no need to be confined to only the bright and immediately attractive. Try the following as a good basic palette to begin with:

Brilliant Blue

Brilliant Red

Vermilion

Yellow Ochre

Lemon Yellow

Black

White

ACRYLICS

There are different trade names such as *Polymer* and *Cryla*. Acrylics are plastic emulsion paints. In manufacture a binder is used instead of a gum which makes acrylics waterproof when dry. Once dry they cannot be dampened and mixed with further layers of colour or on the picture surface. It is advisable to dampen an applicator before loading it with colour. Acrylics have a tendency to dry in a film and may cause an applicator to stiffen in time. An advantage is their value in underpainting.

Acrylics dry more quickly than oils and the warmer and dryer the atmosphere the faster the drying rate. Heavy impasto will dry in three to four hours while thin layers dry in minutes. They can be kept moist by spraying water over the surface. It is preferable to have clear ideas before starting to work since it is necessary to work quickly.

Acrylics can be used to give:

1   Transparent films of colour by diluting them with water. This facilitates glazing which is easier with acrylics than with oils. The length of time taken is reduced. An acrylic glazing medium can be purchased which makes the work easier still. It will also facilitate application of thin collage material.

2   Impasto effects if they are mixed thickly. White added makes them opaque.

3   Interesting textural effects. Paint surface can be built into relief

and the textures developed using a variety of applicators such as knives, spatulas and brushes. This is made all the more interesting when an acrylic modelling or extender paste is mixed with it. Similar to the consistency of putty, it facilitates thick and rich textures.

Acrylics are usually sold in tubes or jars. Since the paint dries fast, and tends to dry out in the tubes, it is difficult at times to get a reasonable quantity from the tube. Try using those produced in jars. The paint tends to remain fresher in the jars though the lids must always be securely fastened after use.

Acrylics can be used on most surfaces including card, hardboard, plaster and canvas whether primed or not. A white primer is available. Rowney *Cryla White Primer* can be used on paper, cardboard, hardboard, plastic, wood and fabric. Fabrics can be rolled without the primer cracking. Previous sizing is unnecessary. The paint is flexible whether it is thin (transparent) or thick (opaque).

Since acrylics dry matt, a plastic-based varnish is available which will give a gloss finish if preferred (a varnish is rarely necessary). An alternative would be to thin colour with a plastic medium instead of water.

Acrylics are useful for compositions which depend on speed of drying and water resistance. They are more expensive and difficult to use than tempera colours. Where they are going to be used, a basic palette to begin with might include:

Titanium white

Black

Cadmium yellow light

Yellow oxide

Chromium oxide green opaque

Ultramarine

Burnt umber

Cadmium red

AQUA PASTO
Winsor and Newton manufacture this colourless gel which can be mixed with water colours. It is:

1 easy to use with a painting knife;

2 transparent whatever thickness is used; and

3 reworkable by wetting it after it has dried.

EMULSION
The household variety of plastic emulsion paint is usually sold in tins.

It can be worked with knives, brushes, rags or rollers (sponge rollers are usually the most suitable). It is similar to other emulsified paints but it is not always waterproof when dry (check manufacturer's instructions).

OILS

Oil colours should be used on a specially prepared canvas, board or paper. The surface of the ground should be coated with size before applying a primer. This will make the surface non-absorbent. Two coats of primer, painted in opposite directions, provide a well integrated picture ground. If a primer is not available, emulsion paint or white undercoat will serve.

The surface of the ground is usually grained to prevent paint from slipping. The smooth side of hardboard can be rubbed with sandpaper before applying the white primer (if preferred the primer surface can be roughened). Surfaces most commonly used with oils are: paper treated with size; some wallpaper off-cuts are suitable – use the reverse of washable and vinyl papers; oil painting paper, sometimes called canvas paper, which is sold in sheets or packets; hardboard, primed; canvas boards; canvas – from fine-grained cottons to rougher textured hessian, stretched and primed. Of these, hardboard and the papers are the most likely to be used, with hardboard providing a durable and reliable surface.

Artists' quality oil colours are the best; Georgian colours by Rowney and Greyhound colours by Reeves are good quality (or their equivalents from other companies); and students' oil colours will be satisfactory for work in school if the foregoing are not available. (See the notes on colour palette, page 75, for a choice of colours.)

The three main thinners or solvents for oil paints are:

1 Oil –usually linseed. It is advisable to keep the use of this to a minimum. Most oil colours are sold ready to use and should not require additions for most purposes. There are two main dangers of excessive use of linseed oil: (a) a greasy surface will result; and (b) colour will darken with the absence of light.

2 Pure turpentine. This prevents too much sheen, which is possible with oils. If used excessively it can give a dry, chalky appearance and reduces the colour brilliance and powers of adhesion.

3 A mixture of pure turpentine and linseed oil. This is called a medium or gel medium. (a) It can be mixed with the colour to produce thin glazes; and (b) it speeds drying by approximately half the time.

Oil colours normally take two to three days to dry (oil oxidises and develops a skin). Very thick paint will take much longer. It is correct to paint: (a) over dry paint; and (b) into wet paint. It is not advisable to paint into sticky or partially dry paint.

Picture grounds or painting
surfaces (Sometimes referred to as supports).

PAPERS

NEWSPRINT   has only minimal use as a surface for painting. It could
be used to make impressions on with sponge or rag, but any attempt to
move colour across the surface will almost certainly result in tearing.
With runny paint it soon becomes saturated. Its flimsy nature causes
thick paint to crack. It is useful for taking impressions of finger
paintings and monprints. Younger children enjoy working on it with
powder colours.

CARTRIDGE   is a versatile paper which can be used for most of the
suggestions made in this book. There are three main surface qualities
from which to choose. In increasing order of roughness they are:
1 hot pressed; 2 cold pressed and 3 rough. Should you wish to paint
with oils, cartridge paper must first be given a coat of size or a
pva binder thinned with water (see the notes on Painting media – Oils,
page 82). The smoother the paper the stronger the colour will remain
after drying. Good quality water-colour paper tends to be expensive.
Try using water colours on a softer paper that has a rough texture.
For most work the weight of the paper should not be less than 95
grammes per square metre. It is a worthwhile experience to paint on
hand-made papers, but these are more difficult to purchase and they
are expensive. Try working on a paper 140 gsm (approximately) in
weight. A really good quality cartridge paper will not be less than
170 gsm. Hot pressed paper is hard and not very absorbent. Paint
can be removed more easily from the surface of smooth paper by
wiping either: (a) while the paper is damp; or (b) when colour is dry,
using a slightly dampened cloth or sponge.

SUGAR PAPER   is made in various thicknesses, textures and colours.
It is particularly suitable for painting with tempera colour in powder
or liquid form. For the suggestions for painting described under
Painting media the paper weight should not be less than 95 gsm.

CANVAS

Oil colours applied with knives or brushes are successful on canvas.
The type of canvas used will depend on individual preferences, from
the finest cotton to coarser hessian. Those bought on stretchers are
usually ready for use; otherwise the canvas, once stretched, will need

a coat of size followed by a primer.

The surface can be prepared for water-based media by applying a mixture of powdered starch, water and a few drops of gum arabic. If transparent water colours are used the texture of the grain of the canvas will be much more important in the final effect. Acrylics can be used more effectively on canvas than on paper. Alternatives might include boards with a canvas texture such as *Daler* board.

BOARDS

In addition to *Daler* board, any of the following could be tried: hardboard, chipboard, essexboard, and plywood. Of these hardboard is the most practical. It can be used for all the methods of painting mentioned in this book. It can be used without priming, but it is usual to coat it with white primer, tins of which can be purchased from most good art suppliers. This reduces the absorbency of the board and provides a white ground which reflects more light. Off-cuts are perfectly good to use and can be further cut to shape and size. The smooth side is the most serviceable and easiest to work on.

Chipboard and hardboard are also useful as drawing boards for stretching papers before painting with water colours.

COLOURED GROUNDS

These will have an influence on colour when transparent or translucent paints are used. Grey and black will tend to neutralise colours. The brilliance of transparent colours will be reduced when painting on a dark or black ground since it will absorb more light than white paper. It may be desirable to have a colour influence throughout a painting. This can be achieved by using a coloured primer or undercoat or mixing quantities of the chosen colour with other colours on the palette. Good colour harmony is obtained in this way, using a 'life-blood' colour. (*Teaching Art Basics* Roy Sparkes, Batsford, London, 1973, page 39.) The colour of the ground is less important where opaque colour is being used or where paint is applied impasto.

TRANSPARENT SURFACES

Perspex and glass are the most likely to be used for painting. An advantage of using a transparent surface is that a sketch or plan can be placed underneath and then seen through the painting surface. This allows painting to proceed with the knowledge that the pencil, charcoal or other drawing media will not be seen in undesirable places in finished work. Oils can be used on glass; and most water-based media mixed with a little pva binder will work successfully on glass or perspex. The binder is advisable for improved adhesion when painting on plastic surfaces.

It is possible to work on both sides so that one complements the other. The 'front' can be painted with foreground details of, for example, a landscape; and the other side with middle tones and greys. The 'back' of the transparent sheet can be painted at any time and not necessarily at the outset as is often advised for most subjects when using water-based media.

OTHER SURFACES
It is worth experimenting with a variety of surfaces:

1   Wallpapers – some of the stronger vinyl papers are capable of holding oil colour as well as being interesting to use with water-based paints.

2   Wrapping papers – mainly for water-colour work.

3   Blotting papers – try the different grades. They will absorb colour quickly. Spraying paint can produce interesting results. Colour areas can be interpreted and developed with felt tip and ball point pens.

4   Mirrors (see the notes on Transparent surfaces, page 84).

5   Fabrics – they can be: (a) stretched on a frame; or (b) glued to a board using size, emulsion paint or a pva binder. There is a wide range of textures and densities to try.

Palettes

STORAGE   Plastic palettes with six or nine wells can be stacked easily and are useful for storing dry powder paint.

MIXING   A flat tray or tile is preferable. Possibilities are formica, ceramic tiles, metal sheets, glass, perspex, plywood, an old dinner plate or a disposable paper palette (waxed or greaseproof papers could be used for oils or acrylics. They are sold as sheets or as strip-off pads). Formica (an off-cut) will make a good general-purpose palette. Wood would have to be sealed with a varnish. Where possible use an appreciable size (30 x 40 cm) especially when working with rollers.

Plaster-mixing

Use approximately 2-3 parts plaster to 1 part water. Pour a sufficient amount of water into a clean bowl – preferably a flexible plastic container since it will be easier to clean. Sprinkle the plaster onto the surface of the water fairly quickly without splashing. When the plaster has formed an island touching the surface of the water, hand stir from the bottom until a lump-free mixture is obtained. In general, when the mix is 1-2 parts of plaster to 1 part water, the plaster will set in 15 minutes. The setting time can be retarded by:

1   Using the minimum of agitation during mixing
2   Adding a tiny amount of sodium citrate to the water before mixing
3   Creating a thin mixture using cold water and a minimum amount of plaster, eg equal parts of water and plaster
4   Mixing vinegar or powder paint with the water before mixing with the plaster

The following methods could be used to accelerate the setting time:

1   Add very much more plaster to water, eg 3 parts plaster to 1 part water
2   Use hot water instead of cold
3   Add plaster to salted water
4   Stir vigorously during mixing

While the plaster is of a creamy consistency it can be poured into moulds or used to make plaster blocks, for example, by pouring it into a thick cardboard box and leaving it to set hard.

There are a number of guidelines to be followed for successful work. Cold water should be used. Always add the plaster to the water, *never* water to plaster. Cover working surfaces and the floor with old newspapers to absorb any plaster that may be spilt. Plaster should never be washed down a sink, it will block the pipes. Use a waste bin to dispose of waste solid plaster pieces. Clean all equipment by washing it with detergent in a bucket.

Primer

Priming makes a surface non-absorbent and receptive to paint. It is usual to apply a white coat which gives greater luminosity to colour painted over it. Boards are the most likely paint supports to need priming, and here it is better to give two or three coats painted in opposite directions to each other, applied when a previous application has dried. It can be applied directly to the board surface or over a coat of size.

Rollers - faults that may develop

Faults that develop with use can be harnessed to effect. The most common are:

1   Warping of the roller surface due to the residue of cleaning fluid after constant use over a period of time. White spirit (the strongest attacking agent) and water are the most frequently used cleaning agents.

2   Too much hand pressure may force rivets outwards at the end of rollers.

3   Swelling may occur at the ends. Colour areas become uneven when using a roller in this condition. The life of a roller will be prolonged if the cleaning fluid is completely wiped off the ends where it tends to collect near the central spindle.

4   The composition rubber covering of some rollers breaks down after repeated use.

5   The surface of a roller may soften and become sticky if used in white spirit.

It is worth noting that a solid rubber roller is much more resistant to the effects of cleaning agents than a foam one.

A roller that has become marked or stained or has warped can be used for textural effects. It is obviously more difficult to control such a roller to make precise statements. However it can still have a use and could be stored separately from rollers in good condition. Experiment will help determine the degree of facility obtainable and the variety of effects that can be produced.

Sponges

If the following suggestions are observed sponges will last well and give good value:

1   They should be washed thoroughly from time to time. At the end of each working session they should be rinsed in clean water as thoroughly as time will allow.

2   When washed, gently squeeze (never wring) them out and hang up or place to dry where air can penetrate the fibres. Do not store them enclosed in a bag or a confined space.

3   It is not advisable to boil sponges since it causes the fibres to harden and deteriorate.

4   Natural sponges deteriorate quickly if used with strong alkaline solutions such as certain cleaning agents and disinfectant. They will become slimy if soap is rubbed onto them.

Spray painting equipment

The quality of spray possible will depend on the choice of diffuser or gun to be used. A sophisticated and expensive air brush will offer the widest range. There is a variety to choose from. Most air brushes have an adjustable nozzle which allows the density of spray to be altered. The finest spray (or smaller points of colour) will allow treatment of restricted or smaller areas and shapes which require a measure of detail; subtle and gentle atmospheric effects and distance — aerial perspective — in landscape; and colour mixing by spraying paint over previous applications, thus allowing the eye to complete the sensation of colour mixing.

An adjustable nozzle will allow the density of spray to be changed from the finest to coarser and larger dots of colour. The latter will be useful for the treatment of larger areas of sky, sea and landscape; action in figures, turbulent seas, cloudy windswept skies; and intense colour areas as when concerned with near objects in paintings employing aerial perspective. The larger the dots of colour used, the more difficult colour mixing may be. It is necessary to stand further back from the finished painting than may be possible in most situations.

The varying degrees of spray density can be directed for certain textural qualities or detail. Most of the smaller areas of detail will probably be painted with a fine spray, but certain subjects will require texture or colour brilliance which can only be acheived using the coarsest of spray applications. Textures of foliage, clothing, walls and rock structures tend to be in this category. The demand for differences of spray density may only be determinable in the event. Practice and experiment are necessary to be able to answer demands as they arise.

A good quality air brush or spray gun will give uniform size of colour dot. Uneven applications of spray are all too often the result of using a less refined spray gun or a diffuser operated by the mouth which at worst approximates to the kind of disparity of size of colour 'dot' obtainable from 'spraying' paint using a toothbrush, which is much more difficult to control.

Some of the most sophisticated air brushes will require a suppressor and a storage tank or a cylinder of gas. The use of gas has enabled manufacturers to make available models that are simpler to use and cheaper. These make spray painting a more likely proposition. Reeves produce *Badger Spray* — to be used in conjunction with an aerosol propellant — which is successful in small scale work. The 'Jet Pack Spray Gun' obtainable from E J Arnold is a self-contained spray gun using an aerosol action. E J Arnold recommend that *Arnold Colourcraft* emulsion or poster paint is put into the paint container and sprayed to cover a surface quickly and evenly. The gun is supplied with power unit and container.

Alternatives to the relatively expensive air brush are a spray diffuser, garden insecticide sprayers and aerosol sprays. The mouth spray diffuser has its limitations (the quality of spray is difficult to control) but will give satisfactory results for beginners. Aerosol sprays tend to be expensive and are also difficult to control. Improvisations could be tried, for instance by using perfume dispensers with rubber bulb attachments. Bernard Cohen used a scent spray '. . . which necessarily made his line relatively wide and soft-focus. Spray techniques have been central to his work ever since'. (Richard Morphet. Introduction in the catalogue to the exhibition of Bernard Cohen's paintings and drawings, 1959-71, at the Hayward Gallery, London, 6 April-14 May, 1972.) When an atomiser (a diffuser that does not provide for the adjustment of spray) is being used the result is usually a coarser texture. Once the kind of spray usual to a particular instrument is known it can be used for special qualities and effects in a painting.

Skill and knowledge in the use of a spraying instrument are important to control the work in hand and to achieve satisfactory results. Spray guns are not easy to control, especially to achieve small areas of definition. It is essential to read manufacturer's instructions carefully before painting. Degrees of refinement in the manufacture will require different measures of control and skill in use. Some delineation can be achieved, depending on three main points:

1 Size of the spray nozzle. An easily adjustable nozzle is preferable.

2 Air (or gas) pressure. Too little pressure and the paint may appear as disparate blobs. Too much pressure and a sudden spurt of colour could be a disturbing surprise. Test the flow of paint sprayed before applying to the picture surface.

3 Distance of the spray nozzle from the picture ground. Held too near the picture surface the paint will collect and lead to puddles of uncontrollable areas of colour. The further away the spray gun or diffuser, the wider the area over which the colour is dispersed, with usually a resultant loss in colour intensity.

If an even covering or dispersal of colour is intended it is essential to move the nozzle parallel to the surface to be painted. A common mistake is to swing the nozzle in an arc leading to an uneven covering and variations in colour density.

Stretching paper

It may be worthwhile to stretch papers that are to be used when painting with water-based media. This will prevent the paper warping when it becomes wet. Soak the paper briefly in clean, cold water. Place it onto a clean drawing board, removing surplus water with a clean sponge. Seal the edges of the paper to the board with brown gummed paper strip, making it air tight. As the paper dries it contracts and becomes taut. This ensures a good, smooth surface to work on. The painting can be removed easily from the board using a trimming knife and a straight edge.

Varnish

There are basically three main uses for varnish:

1 To protect painted surfaces. *Copal* is a hard resin varnish which will give good protection.

2 To revitalise colour that has a flat and dull appearance. *Copal* varnish or a thicker and softer resin such as *Damar* varnish could be tried. The painting must be thoroughly dry before varnishing.

3 Mixed with painting media before application as part of the painting surface. Only small quantities of varnish should be used in this way. It can help to enrich textural qualities in oil painting as, for example, in the work of Keith Vaughan.

It is better to spray water colours with a fixative which can be purchased in aerosol cans or in bottles, when a mouth spray diffuser will be needed. Acrylics should not need varnishing. If desirable an acrylic medium could be used (consult manufacturers' catalogues for details and trade names).

Suppliers

General art materials

Fred Aldous
The Handicrafts Centre
37 Lever Street
Manchester

E J Arnold
Butterley Street
Leeds LS10 1AX

Margros Limited
Monument House
Woking
Surrey

Reeves and Sons Limited
Lincoln Road
Enfield
Middlesex

Crafts Unlimited
21 Macklin Street
London WC2

George Rowney and Co Ltd
10-11 Percy Street
London W1

Winsor and Newton Limited
Wealdstone
Harrow
Middlesex

Dryad
Northgates
Leicester
LE1 4QR

51 Rathbone Place
London W1

Papers

Berol Limited
Oldmeadow Road
Kings Lynn
Norfolk

Green's Fine Papers Division
Sprint Mill
Maidstone
Kent

Falkner Fine Papers
302 Lillie Road
London
SW6 7PU

Paperchase
216 Tottenham Court Road
London W1

Mosaics

Bush Crafts Limited
25-27 Bramley Road
London W8

The Mosaic Centre
83-85 Bondway
Vauxhall
London SW8

Nicholls Clarke Limited
Shoreditch High Street
London E1
(Nic-o-Bond and tile cement)

Proctor and Lavender Mosaics
Solihull
Warwickshire

Photograms

Agfa-Gevaert Limited
Sales Department
Great West Road
Brentford
Middlesex

Kodak Limited
PO Box 66
Kodak House
Station Road
Hemel Hempstead
Hertfordshire

Clays and ceramic equipment

The Fulham Pottery Limited
210 New Kings Road
London SW6 4NY

Newclay Products
14, Annerly Station Road
London SE12

Podmore and Sons Limited
New Caledonian Mills
Shelton
Stoke-on-Trent
Staffs

Potclays Limited
Brick Kiln Lane
Etruria
Stoke-on-Trent
Staffs

Webcot Limited
Alfred Street
Fenton
Stoke-on-Trent
Staffs

Plaster

if not available from general Art
and Crafts Suppliers, try:

Industrial Plaster
British Gypsum
Ferguson House
15 Marylebone Road
London
NW1 5JE

Marbling

Dragon
19 Burbage Road
London SE24

Spray guns and equipment

Hunter Penrose Limited
7 Spa Road
London SE16 3QS

Gerald Stains Limited
Puttridge Works
Fernbank Road
Ross-on-Wye
Herefordshire

Printmaking equipment

including blocks for wood cuts

T N Lawrence
Bleeding Heart Yard
Greville Street
London EC1

Alec Tiranti
70 High Street
Theale
Berks

OVERSEAS ADDRESSES

AUSTRALIA AND NEW ZEALAND
Craft Plus, 89 Latrobe Terrace, Paddington, Queensland

Melbourne Street Arts and Craft Centre, 146 Melbourne Street, North Adelaide

Reeves (Aust) Pty Ltd, 25 Clarice Street, Box Hill South 3128, Victoria

Argyle Craft Suppliers Pty Ltd, 203-233 Playfair Street, Sydney 2000

Souvenarta, 23 Cavenagh Street, Darwin 5790

The Handcraft Centre, Fyshwick Plaza, Wollongong Street, Fyshwick 2069

Smith & Smith Ltd, 73 Captain Springs Road, Takapuna 6, Auckland

High Street Gallery, 93 High Street, Lower Hutt, Wellington

R & C Tingeys & Co Ltd, 30 Manners Street, Wellington

Abernethy's, George Street, Dunedin

Terry's, George Street, Dunedin

Brush-N-Palette Artists Supplies Ltd, Betts Arcade, Cashel Street, Christchurch

SOUTH AFRICA
CNA branches
Helios
For addresses see local yellow pages

Selected Bibliography

Some of these titles may now be out of print but you may be fortunate enough to find copies in your library.

Drawing

Capon Robin   *Introducing Drawing Techniques* Batsford, London
Gettings Fred   *Techniques of Drawing* Studio Vista, London
Jameson Kenneth   *You Can Draw* Studio Vista, London

Kampmann Lothar *Pictures With Crayons* Batsford, London;
  Watson-Guptill, NY
Rottger Ernst and Klante Dieter *Creative Drawing: Point and Line*
Batsford, London; Van Nostrand Reinhold, NY
Walmsley Leo *Approaches to Drawing* Evans, London

Painting

Andrew Laye *Creative Rubbings* Batsford, London; Watson-Guptill, NY

Barker Elver A *Finger Painting in Oils* Van Nostrand Reinhold, NY

Betts Victoria *Exploring Finger Painting* Davies Publications
  Worcester, Massachusetts

Gettings Fred *Polymer Painting Manual* Studio Vista, London

Gore Frederick *Painting: Some Basic Principles* Studio Vista, London

Guptill Arthur L *Water Colour Painting Step-by-Step* Pitman,
  London; Watson-Guptill, NY

Hiler Hillier *Painter's Pocket Book of Methods and Materials* Faber,
  London; Watson-Guptill, NY

Kampmann Lothar *Pictures with Inks* Batsford, London; Watson-
  Guptill, NY

Pope Michael *Introducing Water Colour Painting* Batsford, London

Raynes John *Starting to Paint with Acrylics* Studio Vista, London

Scott Guy *Introducing Finger Painting* Batsford London

Shaw Ruth *Finger Painting* Little Brown, Boston, Massachusetts

Sparkes Roy *Painting Without a Brush* Batsford, London

Szabo Zolton *Creative Water Colour Techniques* Pitman, London

Wehlte Kurt *The Materials and Techniques of Painting* Van Nostrand
  Reinhold, NY

Printmaking

Cooper Mary *Simple Printmaking* Watson-Guptill, NY

Daniels Harvey *Printmaking* Hamlyn, London

Elam Jane *Introducing Lino Cuts* Batsford, London; Watson-Guptill
  NY

Gilmour Pat *Modern Prints* Studio Vista, London

Kent Cyril *Simple Printmaking* Studio Vista, London

O'Connor John *Introducing Relief Printing* Batsford, London

Palmer Frederick   *Monoprint Techniques* Batsford, London

Rhein Eric   *The Art of Printmaking* Evans, London

Rothenstein Michael   *Lino Cuts and Wood Cuts* Studio Vista, London

Russ Stephen (ed.)   *A Complete Guide to Printmaking* Nelson & Sons, London

Weaver Peter   *Printmaking: a Medium for Basic Design* Studio Vista, London

Collage

Brigadier A   *Collage: a Complete Guide for Artists* Pitman, London

Capon Robin   *Paper Collage* Batsford, London

Connor Margaret   *Introducing Fabric Collage* Batsford, London; Watson-Guptill, NY

D'arbaloff Natalie and Yates Jack   *Creating in Collage* Studio Vista, London

Farnworth Warren   *Approaches To Collage* Batsford, London

French Brian   *Principles of Collage* Mills and Boon, London

Haley Ivy   *Creative Collage* Batsford, London; Branford, Massachusetts

Hutton Helen   *The Technique of Collage* Batsford, London; Watson-Guptill, NY

Kampmann Lothar   *Pictures With Coloured Paper* Batsford, London

Richter Hans   *Dada: Art and Anti-Art* Thames & Hudson, London; McGraw Hill, NY

Seitz W C   *The Art of Assemblage* The Museum of Modern Art, NY

Simms Caryl & Gordon   *Introducing Seed Collage* Batsford, London; Watson-Guptill, NY

Stevens H   *Design in Photo Collage* Van Nostrand Reinhold, NY

Mosaics

Berry John   *Making Mosaics* Studio Vista, London

Hutton, Helen   *Mosaic Making Techniques* Batsford, London

Stribling R   *Mosaic Techniques* Allen and Unwin, London

Williamson Robert   *Mosaics* Crosby, Lockwood, London

Relief

Barnsley Alan   *Introducing Expanded Polystyrene* Batsford, London

Cowley David   *Working with Clay and Plaster* Batsford, London

Farnworth Warren   *Creative Work with Plaster* Batsford, London

Farnworth Warren   *Techniques and Designs in Pin and Thread Craft* Batsford, London

Hartung Rolf   *Creative Corrugated Paper Craft*   Batsford, London; Van Nostrand Reinhold, NY

Meilach D Z   *Creating with Plaster* Blandford Press, London

Röttger Ernst   *Creative Clay Craft* Batsford, London

Sparkes Roy   *Exploring Materials with Young Children* Batsford, London

Photograms

Bruandet Paul   *Introducing Photograms* Batsford, London

Haffer Virna   *Making Photograms* Focal Press, London; Hastings House, NY

Kay Alan   *Photography in Art Teaching* Batsford, London; Branford, Massachusetts

Scharf Aaron   *Creative Photography* Studio Vista, London

General

de Saumarez Maurice   *Basic design: The Dynamics of Visual Form* Studio Vista, London

Mayer Ralph   *A Dictionary of Art Terms and Techniques* A and C Black, London

Schwarz Hans   *Colour For The Artist* Studio Vista, London

Sloane Patricia   *Colour: Basic Principles and New Directions* Studio Vista, London